THE
BEANSTALK
JACKPOT$

Jack hit three jackpots by climbing his beanstalk.
You can too.

Pete Geissler

Copyright © The Expressive Press, 2017. All rights reserved. No part of this book may be reproduced or transmitted in any form or by any means, electronic or mechanical, including photocopying, recording, or by any information storage and retrieval system, without permission in writing from the publisher. Competitive Supremacy™ is a trademark of Pete Geissler and The Expressive Press.

ISBN- 13: 978-1542865104
ISBN-10: 1542865107

Books from Pete Geissler

- The Power of Writing Well
- The Power of Being Articulate
- The Power of Ethics, with Bill O'Rourke
- The Power of Dignity
- Leadership for Profitable Sustainability
- Hugging a Cloud
- BigShots' Bull*!@#
- An Accidental Life
- Divorce Can Be Such Sweet Sorrow

Books from The Expressive Press

- Peach, by Jenevieve Woods
- The Little Black Book of Human Resources Management, by Barry Wolfe
- Heydays, by Ray Garra
- Shallow Water Sailor, by Ray Garra
- Rockin' Romance, by Dante Valentino
- VB.Net Web Development, by Dr.CharlesWood

ABOUT THE AUTHOR

Pete Geissler is an outspoken advocate of good communications, behaviors, and thinking as the jackpots that are wealth, happiness, and competitive supremacy--for a successful, enriched life. His books, and hundreds of his articles, speeches, and classes, examine why and how to be articulate, to write well, and to treat people respectfully and ethically. His accomplishments include authorship of a publisher's best-seller, writing more than three million words for businesses, and teaching thousands of businesspersons why and how to be better writers/communicators.

For more:

www.theexpressivepress.com.
www.peteswriteshops.com.
www. petesCV.com.

WIDESPREAD APPLAUSE FOR *BEANSTALK*

Pete Geissler has redefined how businesses and individuals can stand out from the crowd and grow financially and personally—to win the game of a life well examined and lived.

— James David Snyder, Financial Analyst, Executive Wealth Counselors.

By adding communications and behaviors to the traditional elements of competitive advantage, Pete Geissler has paved the way to the far more powerful concept of competitive supremacy for individuals and firms. Take heed, you who want to transform for the better your lives and organizations.

— Paul Spence, Transformation Consultant.

The wonderful thing about this book is that Pete Geissler lives and breathes the three jackpots he posits. He attributes his success as a writer and teacher to his abilities to articulate, and his palpable happiness to his dedication to ethical, dignified behavior. Readers of this book would do well to follow his lead.

— Brandon Haynes, President, Allegheny Financial Group.

I met Pete Geissler at one of his writing seminars some five years ago, and we have become fast friends. I remarked to him once that I cannot imagine anyone not admiring him for his willingness to help others succeed and his ethical lifestyle, which are described in this book. Please read it and reap.

— Donald Nusser, Vice President,
Development and Sustainability, Hatch Mott Consultants.

I love Pete Geissler. He has shown my daughter Jenevieve and me that treating others with the respect they deserve is not a dying art, and that being articulate is a route to success no matter how it is defined. I now teach the same powerful concepts put forth in this book to my students.

— Antoinette Woods DeLorenze, M.Ed.,
Diagnostic Reading Instructor,
Highlands High School and Community College of Allegheny County.

I am happily and prosperously employed in a job I love largely because Pete Geissler taught me the importance of being articulate, particularly to write well. In short, he gave me competitive supremacy, and my employer and I reap the benefits.

— David Larson, Senior Project Manager,
Civil & Environmental Consultants.

If only, if only, if only I had met Pete Geissler years ago--I would have saved literally hundreds, maybe thousands, of hours writing murky proposals and reports that lowered my productivity and profitability. Now I know better. Thanks, Pete.

— Susan Tusick, Founder and CEO,
Tusick Architects Associates.

TABLE OF CONTENTS

PROLOGUE..11
JACKPOT ONE: PAMPER YOURSELF....................14

I. PROTECT, NURTURE, THRIVE............................... 15
1. Rely on Your Most Important Asset: Yourself............. 17
2. Use Your Intelligence for Competitive Supremacy...... 19
3. The Seven Intellectual Standards for Documents......... 21
4. We're Here for Selfish Reasons 24
5. The Nutty Professor Rides Again 26

II. ONE WAY TO LAUGH YOUR WAY TO THE
BANK: BE ARTICULATE... 28
6. 'Writer' Not on Your Card? It Should Be...................... 30
7. Good Communications Can Make You Rich 32
8. Innovation and Information: The Inseparable Keys to
Success 35

III. ANOTHER WAY TO BREAK THE BANK:
ETHICAL BEHAVIOR... 38

9. The One Rule for Reaping the Benefits Of Ethical Behavior..40

10. If Only Ethics Were Simple 43

11. A More Ethical Society? Here's Hope for Skeptics..... 45

12. Ethics, Russia, And the Happy Hazards of Principles 47

13. Can Ethics Affect the Workplace?............................... 49

14. The Squishy Side of Ethics 51

15. Ethics, Dignity, and Conflicts of Interests 53

16. Is A Bribe Always a Conflict of Interest?.................... 55

17. Is Skirting the Law an Ethical Dilemma? 57

18. Another Lovable Rogue, Another Hit Movie? 59

19. A More Ethical Society? Hmm 62

IV. STILL ANOTHER WAY TO THE BANK: DIGNITY FOR EVERYONE, ALWAYS 64

20. Dignity in Basketball, Vulgarity in Politics................ 66

21. Animosity, Verbosity, and Dignity 68

JACKPOT TWO: BE POSITIVE...70

V. HOPE FOR A BETTER WORLD.................................. 71

22. The Rise of Positivity: #1 in a Series......................... 73

23. The Rise of Positivity: #2 in a Series......................... 75

24. The Rise of Positivity: #3 in a Series 77
25. The Rise of Positivity: #4 In A Series 79

VI. HAPPINESS, MARTINIS, AND THE JOY OF RELATIONSHIPS 81
26. Vodka, Spiders, and Story Time 83
27. Vodka, the Cult 85
28. Vodka, Shakespeare, and Job Security 87

VII. AVOID A VERBAL FOG AWARD 89
29. LOL on a Rampage 91
30. Laffable Lingo for Your Amusement 93
31. Hype, O Hype, Thou Art Everywhere 95
32. Spinning as Lying? Does a bear...?............................. 97

JACKPOT THREE: REMOVE YOUR TOXICS..........100

VIII. REJECT BULL*!@#. HERE'S HOW 101
33. Boisterous Bull*!@# : What's a Voter to Do?........... 102
34. Boisterous Bull*! @#: What's A Voter to Do? #2.... 104
35. Boisterous Bull*!@# And the Fallacies of Predictions
.... 106
36. Numbers Don't Lie, Right? 108

37. Apply the Three Sniff Tests 111
38. Reverse These Fallacies of Logic To Rational Thinking
.... 115

IX. HOME SWEET HOME IS MORE THAN A SLOGAN
.... 118
39. To Russia, With Thanks 120
40. To Russia, With Thanks. Part II 123

XI. EMBRACE HUMILITY, ESCHEW ARROGANCE
.... 126
41. Identifying the Culprit: Arrogance 127
42. Identifying and Living the Antidote: Humility 133
43. Project the Future as You Must, but Don't Trust the Outcome 137

TRUE STORIES TO SUPPORT THE JACKPOTS
44. My Muse, The Booze 140
45. Raymond, O Raymond, You'll Never Leave Me 150
46. Bull*!@# Ethics Run Amok 158
47. Jobs And Socrates 161
48. Final Draft: Just Add Tears 164

FURTHER INSIGHTS..173

EPILOGUE: WHAT WOULD JACK SAY?...............174

PROLOGUE

Jack climbed his accidental beanstalk three times to reach wealth + happiness + competitive supremacy™: first he acquired a bag of gold coins, then a goose that lays an unlimited supply of golden eggs, and last a harp that plays by itself. He then chops down the beanstalk and the revengeful giant--a modern metaphor for competitors? — falls to his death. Jack and his mother live happily ever after in plentiful splendor.

The enduring fairy tale originated more than 5000 years ago, and was published in 1734, a mere 283 years in our dim past as I write this.

For almost fifty years — since the early 1970s — I wrote all sorts of marketing materials for all sorts of businesses and individuals, some of which I could call fairy tales. I thought that I was helping them deliver their many messages that would help them sell their products.

In truth, I was helping them to build better, more bountiful beanstalks, to help them hit their own personal jackpots, to create wealth + happiness + competitive supremacy™, which is far more important than a few sales.

I was unknowingly advocating my three jackpots for wealth + happiness + competitive supremacy: pamper yourself, be positive, and delete your toxins.

I support those three jackpots with many essays, blogs, and articles; together, they are the why-to and how-to for your bountiful beanstalk... the beanstalk that you are about to sow, grow, and climb.

If Jack can, you can.

Please allow me to explain my views of wealth + happiness + competitive supremacy:

Wealth is the financial means to provide the basics of a comfortable life, not the excesses of the very rich. Perhaps Aristotle, 384-322BCE, the Greek Philosopher, said it best: '...he is happy who is active in accordance with complete virtue and is sufficiently equipped with external goods...'

Many people believe that wealth and happiness are synonymous, that they are a singular whole, a cause and effect. They are living a fairy tale. 'You can't buy happiness' is a universal truth that manifests itself in many ways, including divorces and suicides among the very rich.

Happiness, according to Immanuel Kant, 1724-1804, a German Philosopher, is far more complex than mere wealth. He describes it as 'the satisfaction of all our desires.' I want to change 'all' — which seems hopelessly idealistic — to 'as many as needed to eliminate misery.'

The classic definition of competitive advantage — a benign idea relative competitive supremacy™ — describes attributes that allow an organization to outperform others such as access to natural resources, low costs, highly skilled labor, and new technology.

This definition is pitifully inadequate. Missing are the abilities to communicate these attributes clearly and concisely, a function of articulate employees, and the unflagging commitment of those same employees to behave ethically at all times and with all people. Also missing is the huge advantage of articulate individuals over their less articulate brethren, a topic that I address in detail in my book *The Power of Being Articulate.*

Combine these attributes with those that are more traditional, and the inevitable result is wealth, happiness, and competitive supremacy for individuals and firms.

You and your organization can start the journey toward a bountiful beanstalk by living the jackpots put forth in this book, then supplement them by referring to the authors I cite above and throughout the text, and in FURTHER INSIGHTS.

— Pete Geissler

JACKPOT ONE: PAMPER YOURSELF

Perhaps Ralph Waldo Emerson, 1803-1882, American essayist and philosopher, said it most famously:

Trust thyself; every heart vibrates to the iron string...great men have always done so...there is a time in every man's education when he arrives at the conviction that envy is ignorance, that imitation is suicide, that he must take himself for better or for worse ...

Norman Vincent Peale, 1898-1993, American author, speaker, and minister, agrees:

Believe in yourself! Have faith in your abilities! Without a humble but reasonable confidence in your own powers you cannot be successful or happy.

Jenevieve Woods, author of PEACH, notes *...we all have a choice on how we can live our lives. No one holds you hostage except you.*

I. PROTECT, NURTURE, THRIVE

Introduction by Jim Browne, Founding Partner and CEO, Allegheny Financial Group

Pete Geissler may be the only person on the globe who traded his car for a bar tab, and I happily take full responsibility.

When I told him, way back in the mid-1990s, that he was his most important asset and he should protect himself by buying a safer car, he 'sold' it to a friend who also owned his favorite bar for a few thousand dollars of booze and food; the ultimate bountiful barter. The bar owner gave it to his son — a former student of Pete's at Carnegie Mellon University — to commute to college some 15 miles away.

A win-win-win, right?

Not so fast. Winners included the bar owner, who saved big bucks by buying a car for pre-tax dollars, his son saved big bucks with extremely reliable and efficient transportation, and Pete saved all sorts of money and aggravation by not trading or selling to an unknown private party.

But Pete also lost: He created an ethical morass that keeps me — and I'll wager Pete, as well — awake at night: Why is it OK for Pete to sell a less-safe car to another person, whether he knows or doesn't know him or her? Isn't that inconsiderate? Dangerous to life and limb?

I know: let the buyer beware and damn the consequences, anything for money, it's the American way. OK, but I know that Pete can't live comfortably with that and he took the middle road: He told the bar owner and his son about my advice and they bought the car anyway. Money ruled.

The real point of this story is that Pete learned that he is his most important asset and he shared his insight with the world by writing about it. Of course, I agreed: If he stops earning, I have less money to manage for him.

1. Rely on Your Most Important Asset: Yourself

I bet that you are not listed as an asset on your personal or organization's balance sheet.

Pity. Your intelligence is your earning power. Ergo, it is your source of assets such as your house, computers, desks, cars, stocks, bonds... the trappings of your life and your spending power. You are the mother lode from which all your other assets emanate.

I came to that rather obvious but elusive conclusion when I first started to work with my asset manager, Jim Browne. One of his first admonishments was to trade my unsafe car for a safer model, as he points out in his introduction. He was protecting his future and mine.

I cannot advise you to sell your car, but I can suggest that you protect your earnings and enhance your balance sheet by writing and speaking well. Many studies, including one of mine, connect being articulate, i.e. communicating intelligently, to enhanced earnings, happiness, and overall satisfaction with life... an impressive return for honing one basic skill.

John Yasinsky, former CEO of GenCorp and several other companies, writes in the Foreword to my book, *The Power of Being Articulate:*

"I first learned the truth and power behind communicating intelligently when I lived in a grimy coal-mining and steel-making town in Pennsylvania, where it was clear that articulate professionals were more successful than the less articulate miners and mill workers. My education continued years later at the top levels of government, business, and academe where I observed power brokers and decision-makers use their considerable skills with language to think clearly, arrive at logical decisions, and convey those decisions clearly to others. And over the years, I saw that my happiest friends and associates were able to communicate clearly with spouses and others with whom they enjoy close relationships".

BTW, business gurus always list being articulate as one of the several traits of effective leaders. One noted that it is the one essential skill for success in business and industry.

2. Use Your Intelligence for Competitive Supremacy

I recently came across a clever definition of an intellect: a person who can hear the William Tell overture and not think of The Lone Ranger. A similar definition is a person who is told to not think of the elephant in the room and doesn't.

Both definitions describe the ability to compartmentalize, to think of one topic and exclude all others, i.e. to concentrate.

Another definition of an intellect is...

You. The person with skills that require intelligence to implement.

An example: I was lunching with a financial manager and I said that we are marketing the same product: our intelligence. When he looked puzzled, I explained: You sell your valuable intelligence about investments, and I sell my valuable intelligence about writing and thinking. We have created our intelligence niches. The common thread is intelligence, albeit of different kinds. That's why your clients hire you to manage their finances, and my clients hire me to either write their marketing and other communications, or to teach them how to do so.

Your language, whether in speaking or writing, reflects your intelligence. Ergo, if you buy the notion that intelligence is your only product, you want to avoid ungrammatical, murky, misleading language such as sentences like this from a newsletter on health: *Eating well and exercising regularly will lower your risk of dying.* Really?

I wrote several articles on the roles and importance of intelligence in creating competitive supremacy for individuals and firms. In one, I noted: *We intuitively know intelligence when we experience it: the person who grasps and analyzes the situation at hand quickly and clearly communicates his or her understandings and conclusions; he or she demonstrates superior perceptions and verbal skills. Whether correctly or erroneously, we label those who don't, can't, or won't as not too bright, slow, and lacking credibility — exactly the labels that will destroy careers and businesses in a heartbeat.*

Please refer to TRUE STORIES and my essay on Steve Jobs and Socrates for more.

3. The Seven Intellectual Standards for Documents

If you agree that intelligence is your only product and is the source of your competitive supremacy, and that your documents display your intelligence most explicitly and often, then it follows that your documents should adhere to these intellectual standards:

1. Clarity: Receivers understand your thoughts after one careful reading/review.
2. Concision/Purposefulness/Relevance:
   Receivers must read only thoughts that are pertinent to meeting their purpose (s); they do not waste time reading extraneous excursions or redundancies.
3. Accuracy/Precision: Receivers can verify or agree with truths.
4. Specificity: Receivers are not required to accept unsupported/unsupportable generalizations.
5. Depth: Receivers grasp underlying rationales that answer why and how questions.
6. Breadth: Receivers comprehend other perspectives and points of view.

7. Logic/Cohesion: Receivers readily perceive that you have arranged your thoughts in an understandable sequence.

I am continuously amazed and amused by documents that cross my desk that fracture one or more of the standards. What do you think of the person who wrote this, which I read in *The London Review of Books*: 'Located in the Botanic Garden in Uppsala, the Swedish Collegium for Advanced Study (SCAS) is a national institute for advanced study." (Do you think that the writer should attend the collegium? My writeshops?)

What do you think of the civil engineer who reported: 'Typical annual volumes reached 8,250,000 gallons per month at a cost of approximately $27,000.' (What is the annual volume? What is the annual cost?)

And how do you feel about a real estate broker who wrote this to convince me to buy a condo: 'The property was originally offered for $235,000. It has since been reduced twice. According to market comparables, it is our opinion that the current listing value is between $240,000 and $250,000.' (What is the price of the property? Do you think I bought it?)

I address how to meet the intellectual standards in my book, *The Power of Writing Well*, and I address why most businesspersons should care about meeting the standards in my book, *The Power of Being Articulate*. The two books complement each other to create compelling competitive supremacy in your professional and social lives.

4. We're Here for Selfish Reasons

'Selfish? Me?' the attendees to my writing classes respond with selfish outrage.

Yup, because this class is all about your wealth and happiness and competitive supremacy — it's all about you, and you thought you were here to learn about writing better.

You are, but writing better is a stepping stone to bigger and better things. Look at your life this way. If you're a knowledge worker, as so many of us are, your only product is your intelligence. Ergo, demonstrations/manifestations of intelligence are your ultimate competitive supremacy in the hunt for a job that is more lucrative and satisfying, or a business that is more productive and profitable.

Your writing is likely the most visible and ubiquitous demonstration of your intelligence or, unfortunately, its lack. Face it, when you read a sentence like this: *Your Annual Wellness Visit is a yearly appointment that is covered **every 12 months**,* you label the writer a brainless, patronizing dummy who is wasting your valuable time, i.e. lowering your productivity by forcing you to read many more words than are needed to make the point.

The #1 cause of happiness is relationships with people with whom you can behave toward and communicate with candidly and kindly... and you can't do that without being proficient with words, the foundation for good writing and speaking. When I think of the many couples I know who divorced or who are constantly bickering on their way to divorce or breakup, I think of people who can't or won't communicate quietly and intelligently to find shared goals.

The bottom line is simply that your words are the tiebreakers, the tipping points, that can make you wealthy (or poor), and happy (or sad), competitive (or not).

Peter Drucker, the respected management guru and author who taught for years at The Claremont Graduate School in California, said with clear insight that, 'The one basic skill in industry is the ability to organize and express ideas in writing and speaking.'

 John Yasinsky, former CEO of GenCorp, echoed Drucker's sage words in my book, *The Power of Being Articulate:* 'Your success in your professional, financial, and personal lives depends to a great extent on your ability to articulate.'

So, is it selfish to write better? Nope. It's smart.

5. The Nutty Professor Rides Again

My students call me nuts when I point out to them that they are professional writers simply because their employers pay them to write.

My students reward me for that insight with an incredulous, 'Not so. I'm paid to design a bridge, clean the air and water, save endangered species, map a site, manage a project — anything but write.'

Not so, again. They admit to spending thirty to seventy percent of their work-time tapping out the words that demonstrate their expertise, aka intelligence, in their main discipline. So, thirty to seventy percent of their pay is for writing, and that qualifies them to be labeled 'professional'.

The thought is centuries old. In the mid-1700s, Samuel Johnson, the great English writer and lexicographer, said, 'Sir, no man but a blockhead ever wrote except for money.'

Sam knew that good writing — writing that is clear, concise, and on-point — is hard work that should be rewarded with hard cash. He also knew that bad writing should be rewarded with disdain.

The subtitle of my book, *The Power of Being Articulate* is *The Thoughtful Leader's Model for Wealth and Happiness.* In the book, I connect vocabulary and writing to success regardless of how success is defined by the reader. I support the connection with compelling statistical, empirical, and anecdotal evidence.

After I explain their status as professional writers, the engineers, scientists, and managers who are my students decide that I am not another nutty professor after all. BTW, you can read in the TRUE STORIES how a beloved teacher started my happy career as a professional writer.

II. ONE WAY TO LAUGH YOUR WAY TO THE BANK: BE ARTICULATE

Introduction by Ed Collins, former Communications Manager, Westinghouse Electric Corporation

I figured that Pete had gone off his rocker when he said that he planned to write a whole book that connects being articulate with financial and social success. Nuts, I said: everyone knows that, it's common knowledge, you'll waste your time, and so on.

Pete showed me statistics dating back to the 1930s that made the connection quite convincingly, then asked me to think of the most articulate people I know, whether rich or poor, happy or sad. I did, and listed a dozen or so top managers where I worked. All are wealthy, seem happy, and are adept with the language. I was beginning to see Pete's point, but, to my everlasting shame, I still couldn't imagine a book on a topic that I saw as pretty thin and tried to dissuade Pete from writing one.

Well, if Pete is nothing else, he's so stubborn that he makes a mule look like a mental gymnast, and he banged out a proposal and sent it to a publisher he had worked with before. The acquisition editor came back with an enthusiastic WOW and *The Power of Being Articulate* suddenly transformed from a germ of an idea to full-fledged book, complete with rave reviews. On a roll, Pete wrote a plethora of essays and blogs on the same topic.

How wrong could I be? How right can Pete be?

6. 'Writer' Not on Your Card? It Should Be.

Even if 'writer' isn't in your title or job description, you're a writer.

We live in a world in which we must write. Your choice of words – in an email, a proposal or report, an article, a blog post, even a text or a Tweet – can open (or close) opportunities to be rich (or poor), happy (or sad), winner (or loser).

We also live in a world in which intelligence, aka innovation, is your only product, your only competitive supremacy. Most people display their competitive supremacy via writing, less by speaking or visuals. Your brilliance is useless unless the world knows it and rewards you accordingly by buying your product or idea, or promoting you to a more responsible position.

Like it or not, you will be judged by your writing – on your style, structure, argument, storytelling, grammar, punctuation, spelling and so on.

I came to these conclusions back in the 1970s when I noticed that my clients in the larger and plusher corner offices lived more comfortably and happily. Discounting any connections between wealth and happiness (there aren't any beyond their shared roots in vocabulary), I wondered why some people were able to reach that desirable human condition, and others weren't. My curiosity first led me to a few simple studies based on observations, and then to some powerful assertions by respected thinkers. To paraphrase, one noted that our ability to use our language determines, to a great extent, the amount of money we will earn during our lives; another noted that our ability to create and sustain close relationships, necessarily based on open communications, determines our happiness.

I am centuries late with that thought. Back in the mid 1400s, Pope Pius II said: *A mighty thing is eloquence ... nothing so much rules the world.*

More recently, in the late 1900s, management guru Peter Drucker said, *the one basic skill needed in industry is the ability to organize and express ideas in writing and speaking.*

I plow deeply into those thoughts in my book, *The Power of Being Articulate: The Thoughtful Leader's Model for Wealth and Happiness.* Caution: reading it could improve your life.

7. Good Communications Can Make You Rich

Managers tend to think of good communications, whether writing or speaking, as simply grammatically and syntactically correct. Others dig more deeply and add conveying the right meanings logically, clearly, concisely. Regardless of definition, when communications are 'good', profits jump; when they aren't, profits plummet.

The reasons profits jump lie in a broader definition of 'good' that includes their results. Good communications:

- Are quickly understood by receivers, thereby eliminating the telephone, email, twitter, and other tag games and meetings with which we are so familiar;
- Assure that receivers act in ways that were intended by senders, avoiding wasteful excursions to the wrong tasks;
- Reinforce positive relationships with friends and customers by being sensitive to their needs and feelings, eliminating the extra-ordinary and very expensive efforts to either bring a friend or customer

back into the fold or develop others to fill in the gap; and
- Are trusted by higher authorities, eliminating editing or, worse, rewriting.

Communications that lead to these results obviously save time and raise productivity and profitability.

How much? is a fair question, and three surveys/studies help with an answer:

The Enterprise Social Network (ESN) concluded that a firm with 100 employees wastes 17 hours a week clarifying bad communications, which they translate to $525,000 a year or $5250 per employee per year.

Gallup notes that bad internal communications cost $26,041 per employee per year, more than five times more than was reported by ESN. So, a firm with 100 employees is losing $2.6 million or more per year.

My survey concluded that bad communications cost between one and ten percent of revenue, or an average of 6 percent. Assuming that the revenue of a firm with 100 employees is about $18 million, the cost per employee per year would be $4800, and the cost to the firm would be $480,000.

Assume that all these costs can be converted to profits by converting all bad communications to good:

	Added profits/employee/year	Added profits /firm of 100employees/year
ESN	$5250	$525,000
Gallop	$26,401	$2,640,100
Geissler	$4800	$480,000
Average	$12,150	$1,215, 000

Yes, converting all bad communications to good is naively hopeful, but 80 percent is surely possible. How? There are only two ways: 1) Hire people who can write, which borders on impossible since the colleges don't teach writing in their professional schools, although some of them say they do; and 2) teach your people to write, which you shouldn't need to do if the colleges did their jobs.

The bottom line: Companies that want to tap into communications as a profit center instead of a loss leader must become educators.

8. Innovation and Information: The Inseparable Keys to Success

Innovation, aka creativity, and information, aka communications, are inseparable and equally important to the success of individuals and firms.

I don't think it's coincidental that Apple and Google top the global charts for highest market values; they either are or are reputed to be highly innovative and extraordinarily communicative to their many stakeholders, including employees and customers. They constantly and frequently introduce new products and services with hard-to-miss fanfare. Who can forget Apple's Super Bowl ads?

Also, not coincidentally, both companies are predominantly in the communications business.

You are too, as I noted in Chapter 6.

I teach in my writeshops that the benefits of good writing extend beyond clear, concise communications to an understanding of thinking ... to exploring new ideas/concepts, aka creativity. In fact, the disciplines of good writing can create new knowledge and insight. I delve into that notion in the intro to PART II of my book, *The Power of Writing Well.* Here's a synopsis:

Writing well enriches every human interaction, and it's a skill that everyone can learn.

But not before we reject the sad truth that in today's society we have neglected the habit of writing clear, concise, purposeful prose ... my definition of 'good'... creating the feeling, the conviction, that careful crafting of words is no longer necessary.

It is, as any person can attest who has lost a contract because of a murky proposal ... lost an opportunity for employment because of an indecipherable resume ... been sued because of a muddy, ambiguous sentence in a proposal or contract ... contested a murky will ... lost a friend because of an insensitive email ... and so on.

The positive consequences of good writing are as endemic.

Yes, people are still hired because they can craft language that reflects intelligence, simply because many of us sell nothing but our intelligence. Contracts are won because the proposal can be evaluated precisely, friendships are created because people find common ground via their language, and lawsuits are avoided when contractual obligations are stated clearly.

The benefits of good writing continue and extend well beyond transmitting information.

Good writing *creates* information, and, therefore, good writing creates intelligence and literally forces that elusive human talent that we have labeled 'creativity'.

In essence, good writing gives our minds a disciplined means of expression and conjuring up that great idea that separates the ordinary from the extraordinary. It is a way to discover what we are thinking.

William Zinsser wrote an entire book, *Writing to Learn,* that delves further into this important reason to write. Susan Horton wrote another, *Thinking Through Writing.* I occasionally refer to either or both in my writeshops.

III. ANOTHER WAY TO BREAK THE BANK: ETHICAL BEHAVIOR

Introduction by Paul Spence, Transformation Consultant and former Vice President, Highmark Health System

I accept total and complete responsibility for Pete's happy addiction to ethics and his copious writings on this complex subject.

Here's why: Several years ago, Pete asked me to write an article on ethics in business for Pittsburgh Engineer magazine. I turned down the opportunity, realistically citing busyness, and suggested that he replace me with Bill O'Rourke, the former President of Alcoa Russia and a dedicated ethicist. Pete did, and voila! a new and enduring partnership was formed. Bill wrote the article for PE and then co-authored a book, with Pete, *The Power of Ethics*. Bill subsequently co-authored a book with colleagues at Brigham Young University, *The Business Ethics Field Guide*.

To be brutally blunt, behaving ethically can prevent doing time in jail, where, unless you've found a way to beat the system, you can't become wealthy or happy. Illegal behavior, the kind that is punished with time behind bars, is tantamount to unethical behavior, and its antithesis is mostly true: Legal behavior *tends to be* ethical, and ethical behavior is *always* legal.

Pete, Bill, and I have become fast friends who appreciate each other's ethical behavior and decry the unethical behavior we see around us. We have become ethics junkies and ambassadors, spreading the word that we can all be more ethical, and it pays off in in all sorts of tangible and intangible ways.

8. The One Rule for Reaping the Benefits Of Ethical Behavior

If it looks wrong or feels wrong, don't do it.

Bill O'Rourke explains how he applied this rule, so disarmingly simple on its face, to the world of business:

"I was in an airport lounge and overheard a group of executives from a competitor discuss their company's plans for increasing market share, obviously valuable information that could advance my career and the sustainability of my firm.

"But, although it is legal to eavesdrop in public venues, it didn't feel right. I approached the group, introduced myself, and explained that I could overhear their conversation and could use the information for competitive advantage. They continued talking as if I weren't there.

"I figured that I had warned them and could use the information as I saw fit. But that didn't feel right either, so I found a seat out of earshot. If my competitors weren't interested in protecting what I saw as confidential information, I would protect them from themselves and me from a situation that I would be ashamed of later.

"When I described this scenario to students during my lectures at various universities, the business majors immediately said that I had done the right thing: the information would likely not influence tactical or strategic plans. The marketing majors, however, chastised me for wasting a golden opportunity to increase revenue and profit, thus proving that their marketing plans and actions were meeting or exceeding goals.

"I see the situation as akin to an athlete who takes performance-enhancing drugs, giving him or her an unfair advantage. The operative word is 'unfair', which is akin to 'unethical'.

"An engineer friend mistakenly received a fax from a competitor that detailed a proposal, including the price — obviously, a slip of a finger on the speed dial. He read the subject line and immediately put the fax through the shredder. He knew that his proposal for the same work was attractive and didn't need the help of subterfuge.

"My rule that 'if it looks wrong or feels wrong, don't do it,' relies for its validity and usefulness on an individual's ethical maturity. Pete Geissler and I define that in our book, *The Power of Ethics*, as: A level of education and experience that permits ethical issues to be recognized as they arise and acknowledges that they must be addressed thoroughly."

"BTW, one benefit of living the rule is the peaceful sleep of a clear conscience."

9. If Only Ethics Were Simple

Responses to ethical dilemmas are typically not a simple matter of choosing right and wrong. Often, it's choosing right and more right.

Bill O'Rourke, in his lectures and classes on ethics at a dozen or so universities and even more businesses, poses ethical dilemmas to attendees and asks for debate:

"One of Alcoa's factories was discharging a small amount of a known carcinogen into the aquifer that supplies water to nearby residents. When it was first found, I could have done the 'right' thing and waited the sixty days the law allows before alerting government officials and residents. Instead I did the 'more right' thing and immediately alerted officials and residents, arranged for shipments of enough bottled water to supply residents for all their drinking and cooking, purchased filters for wells and supply lines, and brought in engineers to oversee their installation."

"My actions cost Alcoa more than a million dollars and were enthusiastically approved by the CEO at the time, Paul O'Neal."

"They also prompted heated debate: Some MBA candidates were unhappy that I would spend stockholders' equity so casually, jeopardizing immediate profitability but totally ignoring the long-term reputation of the company as responsible and, therefore, sustainable. Others suggested that I could have waited the sixty days allowed by law and used the time to find a less expensive solution, totally ignoring any possible effects on the health of residents as they continued to use tainted water. One suggested that I could have done nothing, totally ignoring the law and explaining that the health effects would likely not manifest themselves for years, even decades. You can imagine how quickly I and other attendees with a more mature ethical compass rejected that crassly wrong idea."

"My co-author of the book, *The Power of Ethics,* defines ethics as 'to never harm anyone physically, fiscally, or emotionally.' Alcoa's quick response in this case surely helped to prevent physical and fiscal harm to residents, and I suspect emotional harm as well. BTW, my co-author is quick to turn his negative definition to positive: to help others physically, fiscally, and emotionally."

10. A More Ethical Society? Here's Hope for Skeptics

Bill O'Rourke recently returned from delivering twelve lectures on ethics at four universities and meeting with their students and faculty for in-depth conversations. He exchanged ideas and viewpoints with hundreds of bright, motivated students, and he believes and hopes that they are a fair representation of our future leaders in business, government, and society.

Bill continues in his own words: "I sense that they are infused with integrity, fairness, and the strong needs to be truthful, do what is 'right,' and avoid even the appearance of impropriety. Doing so is sure to reduce the strife, hate, greed, and misrepresentations that are all too common today."

"That won't be easy. Our global society is filled with friction, terrorism, and hate. Greed dominates the motivation of many individuals and organizations, and our political campaigns have become vulgar entertainment. The media, written or broadcast, spin every story to suit their own persuasions, in the process abandoning their charter to report the news with some semblance of objectivity."

"I like to pose ethical dilemmas to my audience to get a closer feel of their thinking. In one, I ask: If you expressly accept a job offer and the next day get a better offer, can you renege on your commitment and take the better job? There's no law prohibiting a prospective employee from rejecting even a signed acceptance, but should your word be your bond?"

"At one university, the answer was easy: the university's policy clearly prohibits reneging except for unusual changed circumstances--e.g. if a close relative becomes ill and you cannot move to the hirer's location. The policy exists to protect the university's and students' reputations for integrity."

"At another university, the students debated the issue heatedly. Some students argued that companies and employees are no longer loyal to each other, so it's Ok to renege, which perpetuates the disloyalty that nobody wants. Others argued that if it is legal (or not illegal) to renege, then it's Ok to do so. As long as you don't break any law – your behavior is just fine.

"Which inevitably brings up the ageless issue of the law and ethics and the ageless question: if a given situation is legal, is it ethical by definition? Of course not! See the TRUE STORIES for a timeless example."

12. Ethics, Russia, And the Happy Hazards of Principles

Bill O'Rourke muses about ethics in a hostile environment:

"When I was President of Alcoa Russia I organized a day-long conference on leadership for my top reports, most of whom were Russians unfamiliar with our culture.

"The word got out and a friend and senior Alcoa executive in London asked if she could attend. Of course, I said yes, I'd love to have her. She went about the frustratingly lengthy business of getting a work visa, found that she couldn't in time for the meeting, settled for a tourist visa despite my advising her not to, and flew into the Rostov airport."

"When asked by the Russian officials about the purpose of her visit, she said that she planned to tour the Alcoa plant. 'Sounds like business', they said, and threatened to detain her. She called me and asked me to tell the officials that her visit was strictly sightseeing. I refused to lie."

"She was promptly shackled and escorted to the nearest jail. I made a few discreet phone calls and she was transferred to a comfortable hotel room with an armed guard stationed at her door 24/7. Two days later she was escorted to the airport and told to leave."

"She's been cool to me ever since, says she respects me for sticking to my principles but can't be my friend. I know I did the right thing and am sorry that she doesn't see it quite that way."

"The incident reminded me of when I landed in Russia several years earlier. A minor official told me to put fifty dollars in my passport and hand it to the customs official or I would be detained in a locked room. If I didn't have the cash on me they pointed to a nearby ATM. I refused and was detained for nine hours before they realized that I wasn't going to pay no matter how long I was locked up."

"I relate that vignette and many others in a chapter in the book, *The Power of Ethics*, that I co-authored with Pete Geissler. When you read it, I'm betting that you'll thank your lucky stars that you live in the USA, despite its warts."

13. Can Ethics Affect the Workplace?

I was dining with a neurosurgeon and the CEO of a mid-size consulting firm and we meandered to the subject of ethics in our respective professions.

"Ethics in neurosurgery means being as close as possible to certainty--the certainty that I am doing what is best for my patient regardless of the time it takes. The other day I was operating and, despite extensive prep, I became unsure that I was making an incision in exactly the right place. I backtracked and restudied the X-rays and ignored my colleagues who were urging me to hurry--another patient was waiting and we need to meet our billing target."

"Ethics in my engineering consulting firm means no cheating, ever. We will not cheat any of our stakeholders-- our clients, suppliers, our employees, our communities-- by lowering the quality of our work or overcharging. Doing so and you're outta here, now."

"Ethics in my communications firm means to not lower the quality of my work and not tolerating clients who ask me to do so. I was asked recently to improve documents published by a large insurer and, after reviewing a few, I proposed the total re-write they need for a quality product and estimated the cost. My client asked if I would do a 'light edit at a lower cost'. I walked away.

"Why do we insist on high standards for ourselves and those around us?" I asked during the dinner.

My neurosurgeon friend said that his ethics allows him to sleep at night by avoiding the nightmares of mistakes and lawsuits; my CEO friend said that his ethics is the route to the lower costs of repeat business, sustainability, and higher profitability; and I said that my ethics enables me to work with like-minded clients who are also my friends.

At the risk of being simplistic, I think that ethics in any business, or in any human interaction for that matter, boils down to trust. Customers trust suppliers to deliver the quality products they promise, suppliers trust customers to pay a fair price for value received, employees trust employers to honor agreements and vice versa, and so on.

BTW, this conversation kicked off when the CEO asked me which of my books I was most proud of writing. I said *The Power of Ethics*, and pulled a signed copy from my briefcase and gave it to him, saying that there seems to be a plethora of unethical behavior around the world and maybe this book can turn the tide one reader at a time. I also noted that I wrote the book with Bill O'Rourke, a former executive at Alcoa and now worldwide lecturer on ethics who I am busting with pride to call my friend.

14. The Squishy Side of Ethics

I don't get it.

The Pittsburgh School Board hired a superintendent and then found that he had plagiarized and lied on his resume.

A local paper reported that members of the school board, and their outside attorney, were "scrambling' over what to do.

Bull*!@#

I've taught at two major universities and both cite plagiarizing as grounds for immediate, irrevocable dismissal. I'd bet that most schools live by that same standard. So, why doesn't the board dismiss the new guy ASAP? Does he live by a different and more lenient set of rules?

I don't know. I do know that if he somehow gets the job, the board is condoning lying and stealing. What a great role model for our youth!

I also wonder: How did this guy pass the vetting process, especially when it is so ridiculously easy to spot plagiarism using apps specifically for that purpose. I know firsthand.

When I was teaching at Duquesne University's Graduate School of Environmental Science and Management, a student's writing suddenly improved noticeably. To catch the plagiarism, all I had to do was log on and type in a suspicious phrase or two. I did that three times in my twenty-year career in academe, and two of the three students were expelled. I pleaded with the dean to forgive the third, a student from a poor country in Central America who lives by different rules.

I often wonder: Did I do "the right thing"? Did I set a double standard? I can argue both sides of those questions.

In the book I wrote with Bill O'Rourke, *The Power of Ethics,* we point out that many ethical dilemmas can be resolved by choosing one of several "right things". Resolving a dilemma could very well boil down not to a clear-cut right vs. wrong, but a fuzzy right vs. right.

15. Ethics, Dignity, and Conflicts of Interests

"People struggle with conflicts of interests; they just don't get it. Yet it's the most common ethical dilemma."

So says Dr. Bradley Agle, the George W. Romney Endowed Professor at Brigham Young University and the co-author of the first ever field guide to ethical behavior. He relates a recent event to prove the point:

"A colleague and I each received a box of steaks worth about $250 from Dow Jones, the publisher of the popular stock market averages and The Wall Street Journal. The steaks were, on the surface, a harmless 'thank you' for buying literally hundreds of subscriptions for students.

"My colleague used the steaks to host a backyard barbeque; I sent mine to the local food bank, and I'm no vegan. Why? Accepting the steaks could very well compromise my objective judgment in the future. I might favor Dow Jones when another supplier might be more appropriate ... a clear conflict of their interest in selling more publications to me and my interest in buying the best publications for my students.

"It's also bribery and insulting. I am insulted that Dow Jones would think so little of my character that I would accept a bribe. I see no dignity in that."

I ran into a similar ethical dilemma a few years ago. After lunching with a client (an acceptable form of bribery in today's business world?), he suggested that we look at the fine china at a nearby boutique, noting that he and his wife were in the market for new place settings. As we strolled through the many displays, he pointed to one particularly expensive set and said, "My wife would love that."

The conflict was clear: He wanted to save a few hundred dollars at the expense of his reputation, and I wanted to book more of his business, at the expense of my reputation.

I recognized the bait, but didn't bite. Instead, I told the story to several other clients in the same firm, and they reacted as I hoped: "It's about time somebody gave the comeuppance to that shyster. He tarnishes all of our reputations."

He never asked me to work for him again, but others in the company showered me with work. I can look at myself in the mirror, and I hope that he can as well. Do you think that he can?

16. Is A Bribe Always a Conflict of Interest?

Yes, in my view.

Conflicts of interests rear their unethical heads whenever personal interests influence, or *appear* to influence, official duties. Now substitute 'Bribes' for 'Conflicts of Interests'. The meaning hasn't changed.

In my previous blog, I related how Dow Jones tried to influence two professors with steaks, hoping to influence future purchases of publications; and I related how my client tried to influence me to buy his wife an expensive set of dishes in return for additional business. Both were conflicts of interests and bribes.

Conflicts and bribes extend beyond expensive gifts. A Bishop placed political signs in his yard, hoping to influence, aka bribe, voters to pull the same levers as he does. In doing so, he ventured far beyond his official duties and blatantly fractured a timeless political principle, the separation of church and state.

A top manger hired his wife as a Vice President, justifying his actions by saying that she is the most qualified candidate, bypassing and eroding the morale of others in the firm who were more experienced and equally or more qualified. He might be correct, but he exuded the *appearance* of nepotism, a peculiar type of ethical failure that is sure to enrich his family's coffers.

A related anecdote: A high school soccer coach played his son a disproportionately high number of minutes, eroding the morale of other players. Was it ethical for him to do so? Should he have played his son fewer minutes? Assuming his son was an outstanding athlete, would either course of action be ethical?

These kinds of ethical dilemmas are *unethical requests from authority figures,* and they raise serious questions: Does the authority figure have the right to act as he/she did? Does the act comply with the stated ethics and other policies of the organization? Is what the authority figure is trying to accomplish self-serving?

17. Is Skirting the Law an Ethical Dilemma?

Twenty years ago, a modestly wealthy woman retained me to research ways to shield her assets and herself from a vengeful husband she was planning to divorce.

It was astonishingly easy.

I called a friend, the CEO of a financial consulting company who I figured would know about but never be part of laundering and the like, and he put me in touch with a lawyer who specialized in it. We met over lunch at his posh club, and the conversation went like this:

"She and I fly to Zurich, drive across the border to Lichtenstein, and I introduce her to the manager of the State Bank. He opens a numbered account; she deposits a few hundred thousand to show good faith and wires the rest of her assets when she returns to the states."

"Won't her husband know that she did this? Won't the IRS?"

"Yes, but it won't make any difference. Her husband can't access the account and the IRS won't care as long as she pays the proper taxes. However, she is hiding assets that enter into a civil case, and that isn't cause for extradition from many countries. She'll have to move to avoid jail and losing all her assets to her husband. I suggest Portugal or Paraguay, but never Canada or England."

When the lawyer and I parted, he said, "We never had this conversation, right? I could be disbarred for suggesting what could be considered unethical."

Yes, it could be and, frankly, it should be.

In our book, *he Power of Ethics,* Bill O'Rourke and I list thirteen ethical dilemmas. Number five is, "Skirting the rules and breaking the law." We examine that dilemma conceptually in an appendix and anecdotally in two chapters. In the appendix, we note that "When ethics collapses (as it did in the anecdote above) the law rushes in to fill the void. Why? Because regulation is essential to sustain any kind of human experience that involves two or more people."

I reported my findings to the woman who retained me, and recommended that she settle amicably with her husband. I have no idea if she did or not, and don't care.

18. Another Lovable Rogue, Another Hit Movie?

A recent story in the local newspaper caught my imagination and offended my sense of ethics.

Seems a former president of a county bar association masqueraded for a decade as a practicing estate lawyer and partner in a law firm ... without a license. She was eventually convicted of forging transcripts from a prestigious law school that attested to her stellar academic record, practicing law without authorization, and tampering with county records. Who vetted her?

Her story reminds me of two hit movies, the first from 2002: *Catch me if you can.* It starred Leonardo DiCaprio as a con man who managed to land jobs as an airline pilot, surgeon, and lawyer by using his amazing talents for forging documents, sweet-talking many people who should have known better, and mis-directing his superior intelligence. He was finally caught by an FBI agent played by Tom Hanks.

My second movie is from 1953: *Captain's Paradise.* It starred Alec Guinness as a carefree ship's captain who shuffles like a commuter bus between wives in ports on opposite sides of the Mediterranean, changing his identity from a wild party-goer to a staid family man as needed. He was finally exposed when the wives accidently talked to each other and compared notes.

I harbor a love-hate relationship with lovable rogues who somehow hoodwink the high and mighty. Perhaps the most famous is Don Juan, the fictional womanizer who was created by an obscure Spanish playwright named Tirso de Molina way back in 1630. The Don lured so many ladies into his bed that he lost count and took great delight in hoodwinking and cuckolding their husbands, many of them stuffy, complacent royalty. The Don was so popular that Wolfgang Amadeus Mozart, he of the movie *Amadeus* and reportedly a rogue himself, composed a best-selling opera in his name: *Don Giovanni*. The Don lives today in the popular sitcom, *Two and a Half Men*.

When I shed my fantasies of the joys of carefree life and enter the cold light of reality, I realize how totally unethical false identities are, how they are just plain lying.

In our book, *The Power of Ethics,* Bill O'Rourke and I delineate the nine habits of ethical power. The fifth is: *Tell the truth, the whole truth, and nothing but the truth.* The second is *Consider the consequences of your actions.*

I know that the fake lawyer did not tell the truth and probably did not consider the consequences. Do you think Steven

Spielberg, the director of *Catch me if you can,* would be interested in her story?

19. A More Ethical Society? Hmm ...

I'm convinced that all sentient people want a more ethical society, one that is without corruption, lying, arrogance and the like. Today's newspaper makes me hopeful, hopeless, and perplexed.

On the hopeful side, I applaud James Patterson, the popular mystery writer, for encouraging reading by donating twenty-five thousand copies of his children's book to Baltimore schools ... Queen Elizabeth for celebrating her record-setting longevity on the British throne with the quiet dignity that is her trademark ... and the anonymous person who returned a cell phone to a friend who had left it in a baseball park's restroom.

On the hopeless side, I am appalled that Zimbabwe has backed off its insistence that the dentist who shot Cecil the lion be extradited, explaining that it wants to protect its lucrative hunting industry... I decry the political speech coach who has pleaded guilty to ethical violations ... and I cannot stomach or fathom still another Priest who has been accused of paying young boys for sex.

On the very, very hopeless side, I cannot remember being as incensed as I was after seeing the video of two Texas high school football players wantonly and cowardly attack a referee from behind. After one clipped him at the back of his knees, the other piled on, I suppose to be certain that the poor guy wouldn't get up and fight back. The school's response so far has been to suspend the students and reprimand an assistant coach for remarks that supposedly ignited the incident. I was hoping, naively I admit, that this display of senseless brutality be the tipping point toward deleting from our society football and other violent sports, or at least changing the rules of conduct. LOL.

Then, on the perplexed side, I applaud the person who returned a purse to a shopper who left it in her cart and boo this same person for stealing the $550 that was in it. .. and I applaud Hillary Clinton for finally confessing that she was wrong to waffle, hedge, lie and now "take full responsibility" for her handling of emails. I boo her for not telling the truth as soon as the story broke.

In our book, *The Power of Ethics,* Bill O'Rourke and I contend that the core of ethical behavior is personal integrity and the cause of unethical behavior is arrogance. You can spot the truth in that contention in the above snippets.

IV. STILL ANOTHER WAY TO THE BANK: DIGNITY FOR EVERYONE, ALWAYS

Introduction by Joe Massaro III, President and CEO, Massaro Construction Group

Pete and I met through a mutual friend who has for years admired the dignity with which my grandfather and father before me have treated our employees and others. I only hope that I can carry on their tradition.

Our mutual friend told Pete, and Pete mailed me his book, *The Power of Dignity*. I read and admired the book — it resonated, as the saying goes, to the extent that I even recognized some of the businesspersons that Pete profiled and wish I had been one. I called Pete, commented that he seems like a compassionate person, and asked him to lunch to discuss a book I wanted to sponsor.

Pete and I conceived *PEACH*, the book, at that lunch, and we launched it several months later. I find it amazingly fitting that the book is about a teenage girl with disabling and life-shortening disease who searched for dignity throughout her life. She describes, in her own words, how it feels to be 'silent and invisible in a crowd.' In other words, she describes how it feels to be treated without the dignity she and everyone deserves.

20. Dignity in Basketball, Vulgarity in Politics

Candidates for political office could learn a lot about dignity from Kris Jenkins and Nate Britt.

Ten years ago, Nate Britt's family legally adopted Kris Jenkins, and the brothers played basketball against and with each other for years. On Monday, April 4, Nate's University of North Carolina and Kris' Villanova played for the national championship, and Kris hit a three-point buzzer-beater to win the game.

Nate could have responded with sour grapes. Instead, he told Kris how happy and proud he was for him.

I for one would respect Hillary Clinton if she had congratulated Bernie Sanders on his primary wins. Instead, Hillary accused Bernie of showing his true colors and running for the presidency (to which I reacted with an incredulous 'when wasn't he?'). And Bernie can't get off his mantra that Hillary 'lacks the qualifications and intelligence to be president', effectively calling her 'stupid'. Can you imagine Kris and Britt insulting each other like that?

I would respect Trump if he had not officially added Kasich to his list of 'no-action, all-talk politicians', and instead credited Kasich for policies that helped to create some 400,000 jobs in Ohio. And I might respect Kasich if he had not called Cruz 'Lyin' Ted,' a nickname originally coined by Trump.

While researching and writing my book, *The Power of Dignity,* I was fortunate to discover leaders in a variety of organizations who actually understand and practice the awesome power of dignifying and respecting the people who depend on the organizations for their livelihoods, and on whom the organizations depend on for their existence — the perfect win-win.

The leaders of those organizations are convinced that dignity is the root cause of efficiency and sustainability. They know that dignity is a powerful management tool for competitive supremacy, perhaps the most powerful in their vast toolbox. They also know that, in a perfect world, we would all behave 24/7 with the dignity and respect we all deserve.

Kris Jenkins and Nate Britt know that intuitively. Our political candidates?

21. Animosity, Verbosity, and Dignity

Our leaders in DC conjure images of Nero, the emperor who supposedly fiddled while Rome burned and his subjects screamed as they were barbequed and baked.

President Obama and Congressman Mitt McConnell are fiddling, not with their Strads, but with words while we citizens await, according to Obama, the first strike of a war of some type. Regardless of type, we can expect to sizzle and it's déjà vu all over again. (With apologies to Yogi Berra.)

The discussion-in-name -only of the Iran Nuclear treaty has degenerated into name calling, finger-pointing, and downright nasty and unfounded accusations, none of which has anything to do with the only issue: Will it or won't it improve the security of our country and the world.

Obama accused opponents to the treaty of being war mongers when he said: '(Their)...mindsets are characteristic of a preference for military action (a euphemism for war) over diplomacy.'

To which McConnell retorted by calling Obama a demeaning liar: 'Let me repeat my call for the president to shelve those talking points no one believes and resist those insults no one deserves so we can aim higher — and rise to the moment together.'

Attacking a person instead of the issue is a fallacy of thinking called *ad hominem;* it is way too common in politics and elsewhere in our society, we all should have outgrown it when we left he kindergarten playground and its name calling for more mature pastures.

And it is below the dignity we should expect of our leaders. In fact, it is and should be below the dignity of everyone everywhere. I define dignity in my book, *The Power of Dignity* as the state of being worthy of honor and respect; worthiness, high regard or estimation; self-respect; importance.

Do Obama and McConnell fit the definition?

JACKPOT TWO: BE POSITIVE

Introduction by Martin E. P. Seligman, Ph.D., author of Authentic Happiness and Fox Leadership Professor of Psychology at the University of Pennsylvania

Like many fellow occupants of the chilly half of the positivity distribution, I comfortably consoled myself with the excuse that how I felt didn't matter, because what I really valued was interacting successfully with the world. But feeling positive emotion is important, not just because it is pleasant in its own right, but because it causes much better commerce with the world. Developing more positive emotion in our lives will build friendship, love, better physical health, and greater achievement.

V. HOPE FOR A BETTER WORLD

Introduction by Deidra Czapko, telecommunications consultant

I was Pete Geissler's assistant for some fifteen years and we still, more than ten years since I left to work in telecommunications and he moved on to more teaching and writing books, get together every month or so, usually over a light lunch. We enjoy reminiscing about the good old days when we worked together to satisfy clients and enjoy our creativity. They were happy and productive years that enriched our lives in many ways.

In part because of those years--and in part because of my deep faith-- I honestly believe that there is far more good in the world than our media report, dedicated as they are to the 'tears and fears' that they are convinced sell papers and air time. I reject and resent their pessimism, and instead prefer to look on the bright side of human nature and am convinced that it will prevail.

Pete agrees, as you can read in his books *The Power of Ethics* and *The Power of Dignity.* In them, he calls for a more ethical and dignified society and profiles influential people who think along the same lines. He also is constantly searching for everyday people and events that add even more hope for a better world, and writes about them for others to emulate.

22. The Rise of Positivity: #1 in a Series

Seems to me that we are bombarded with negativity in our news--fires, murders, slanderous statements, and just plain vulgarity. 'Tears and fears' rule the airways and printways.

So I'm switching to positivity by telling you about my Saturday last. I hope that you find the change refreshing.

My soos--significant other, opposite sex-- and I drove some 50 miles to a favorite restaurant where our forty-something server, Tom, aka jar head for his stint in the Marines, told us that he coached midget sports. So I naturally asked him what he thought of the Steelers' hiring of Michael Vick, a hot topic at the moment. He said that he was unhappy that the ball club's management had apparently sold its ethics to the money that emanates from winning games at any cost.

So, naturally, I asked him what he said about the Vick-bit to his young charges. He replied that he takes the high road by teaching--insisting on-- sportsmanship, and, above all, respect for teammates, opponents, and all life in equal, massive doses.

Then, on the drive home, a strange icon flashed on the data screen in my almost-new, hi-tech car. I pulled into a dealership and, by amazing coincidence, flagged a mechanic — the Service Manager? — as he was leaving the service bay. He immediately grasped the situation, drove my car into the service area, and returned fifteen minutes later with my keys and a clear explanation of the problem and how he had fixed it.

This good Samaritan declined my offer to pay the dealership or to tip him for his prompt service. When I quietly insisted that I owe him something for not only fixing the problem but also relieving my anxiety, he merely asked that I bring my car to this dealership the next time it needs service.

Someday I will write sequels to my books *The Power of Ethics* and *The Power of Dignity*. They will be nothing but Positivity. Please stay tuned.

23. The Rise of Positivity: #2 in a Series

I am a director of a small non-profit, Opera Theater of Pittsburgh, OTP, and I am constantly awed by the positivity of our President, Dr. Gene Myers. He remains upbeat despite OTP, like many non-profits, continually being 'one check away from either boom or bust'.

Not surprisingly, Gene devotes inordinate time to finding new money and to monitoring the use of old money. He meets with bankers and fund managers to convince them to donate, and he presides quietly and, at times, humorously, over board meetings that are largely devoted to analyzing expenditures relative to income, aka cost/benefit analyses.

He lives by two management principles: Never, ever compromise the quality of performances to save a buck; doing so will assure OTP's untimely death. And always be transparent so that all stakeholders know OTP's condition and direction.

Gene is retired Distinguished Professor Emeritus at the University of Pittsburgh Medical Center, where he was Chairman of the otolaryngology department. He is a renowned surgeon who travels globally to train doctors how to treat cancer of the neck and head, his specialty. He works with Brothers Brother to find the instruments needed to set up clinics in developing countries, then travels there to train medical and management personnel. He admits to having visited 96 countries, many more than once. For example, he has lectured in Brazil 26 times, and in Taiwan 'too many times to count'.

A recent example: He spent three weeks in Eastern Europe lecturing at various medical schools, then stopped in Philadelphia on the way home to give the commencement address to the graduating class of his alma mater, Temple University Medical School.

I met Gene too late in life to profile him in my books *The Power of Dignity* and *The Power of Ethics*. He belongs in both. I assure you he will be in the sequels.

24. The Rise of Positivity: #3 in a Series

My students tell me that my unrelentingly tough stance on the evils of bad writing is negativity. In fact, it is positivity in the sense that the first step in crafting good writing is to identify the bad and improve it to be good.

I love and applaud good writing, and when I find it I rush to share it with my many like-minded friends and students.

I especially like the opening lines of books, stories, and essays that prod me to read deeper into the piece and that somehow connect to my life.

Consider this opener to a short story by Tess Gallagher: *They say that my great grandfather was a gypsy, but the most popular explanation for his behavior was that he was a drunk.*

Oh my, after reading this juxtaposition of two unrelated thoughts, I couldn't wait to read about this guy's life and behavior as a gypsy and a drunk. Could it be because I had an uncle who fit the same mold? Uncle Ernie sailed the oceans during World War Two, delivering supplies to our troops on the European fronts. He survived the war, but not a bar brawl in Los Angeles some ten years later, which was surprising: he was the fleet's champion boxer.

Tess continued: *How else could the women have kept up the scourge of his memory all these years, had they not the usual malady of our family to blame? Probably he was both a gypsy and a drunk.*

Indeed, how could I have kept the memory of Uncle Ernie for the past sixty years if I hadn't admired a mysterious vagabond and rogue whose life bordered on myth?

Then I read this opening line to a small book of essays written by Tim Hayes, a friend and fellow writer of corporate information: *Big bird is really a dragon.*

Huh? I know big bird and he (?) ain't no dragon. So I read on: *In the 1950s, Jim Henson created a seven-foot high marionette/puppet dragon... A few years later, Henson and others built on that experience and created Sesame Street and Big Bird.* (Please forgive my paraphrasing,)

You can read the entire tale in Tim's book *Jackass in a Hailstorm*, itself quite enticing. And, if you're interested in good communications and especially good writing, please read my books *The Power of Being Articulate* and *The Power of Writing Well*. Thanks

25. The Rise of Positivity: #4 In A Series

Jim Browne's favorite word is *patience* and his favorite sentence is *we're not for everyone.* They define his positivity.

Jim is a founder of Allegheny Financial and my adviser. When the financial markets trend downward, he counsels patience and reminds me that, historically, the markets swing down and then recover three times a year and will soon trend up. When I ask him how long it will be before the uptrend--how he defines *soon*--he replies *patience.*

Ok, that's pretty vague, but it also is realistic. Nobody has ever been able to accurately predict short-term swings in the markets. It also shows positivity, the optimism that downs will soon be ups if we are patient enough to let it happen. Easy to say, hard to do, right?

Soon is also not very satisfying for some investors looking for quick profits and the excitement of roller-coaster rides in the markets, which prompts Jim's favorite sentence: *we're not for everyone.* That one short sentence defines the unwavering focus of the firm.

When Jim and I meet every six months to review my portfolio, I invariably leave feeling happy with my lot in life and optimistic about the future, which invariably prompts me to remind Jim that he manages my comfort, not just my portfolio. I will never forget Jim's initial advice to me some twenty years ago: sell my unsafe car and buy a safer one. Why? I am my most important asset. Aren't you yours? (See Chapter 1 for more.)

I think of patience and positivity as birds of a feather. Patience certainly demonstrates a strong faith that the future will be better than the past, which is perhaps the ultimate positivity.

BTW, Jim and his firm are chapters in my books *The Power of Dignity* and *The Power of Ethics.*

VI. HAPPINESS, MARTINIS, AND THE JOY OF RELATIONSHIPS

Introduction by Don Nusser, Vice President, Hatch Mott Engineers

If common interests are the bonds for the friendships that are the primary cause of happiness, then Pete and I will be close friends for life.

When I first walked into his writing class, I knew that we had one thing in common: we were the oldest in the room. My gray hair and his wrinkled face proved it.

Then, as the class progressed and we talked, we found that we shared a love of clear, concise language and for clear, crisp vodka martinis. A week later, at the next class, Pete handed me three books on the history and mystique of our drug of choice, explaining that the books, elegant in their own ways, were among his cherished possessions. Then, after class, we huddled at the nearest bar and explained to the bartender how to make the perfect martini and told stories and jokes about this drink that has become a cult. Thank you, James Bond.

Since then, we try to meet once a week and, often, try out a new vodka--we are not purists and eschew gin-- that we've heard may be the cleanest and crispest of all. If we find one we particularly like, we declare it the 'house vodka'. So far, I'd guess that we've discovered at least a dozen that deserve our top accolades.

So, here we are, years later, still tippling happily and writing about it. May it never end. Skoal and prossit!

26. Vodka, Spiders, and Story Time

On Sunday, October 4th, I celebrated National Vodka Day with my cocktail of choice: grain vodka with a drop or two of the driest Italian vermouth, and no fruit to mar the taste of the tasteless libation that has been called "the water of life."

Vodka Day reminded me of a story (see TRUE STORIES) I wrote about sipping vodka as a spider descended directly over my glass from an overhead balcony. It finally fell in the icy nirvana and drowned. "No better way to go", I said to a friend and fellow vodka aficionado. "As W. C. Fields said, 'Drown in a cold vat of whiskey? Death, where is thy sting?"

I was also reminded of a bartender in a DC hotel with the memory of an elephant. Every two years, when I stayed at the hotel while at a convention, I would walk into the bar and he would greet me by name and ask: "The same? Vodka on the rocks, no fruit?" He obviously had not drunk enough of it to destroy the brain cells that count in his profession. (See my book, *The Power of Dignity*, for the full story.)

Life with vodka has been good for me, as I say in the opening line of my spider story: 'It's been far more glad than sad during the past 60 or so years'. Yeah, I've been drinking it that long and I started at the legal age but before I was shaving regularly and when girls were still a mysterious curiosity. For you who are counting, that puts me well into my eighties and I'm still enjoying fermented potato, grain, and grape.

Enjoy.

27. Vodka, the Cult

National Vodka Day has come and gone, but the memories of the vodka martini I relished that day linger. Its ability to rapidly improve my mood after my favorite football team blew a close one, the growing and glowing sense of peace with myself and the world, and the ephemeral confidence that I could solve insoluble problems confronting friends, family, and society.

So, to share and spread the mood with all mankind, I am declaring this week to be National Vodka Martini week. My many vodka-drinking friends would scoff: every week is vodka mart week for them, as it is for me. We are a cult of appreciators, albeit in different ways.

One, for example, drinks the least expensive brand, convinced that all vodkas are created equal and that price is irrelevant. I think he's misguided. Another drinks nothing but potato vodka simply because his doctor told him years ago that it is the least harmful, i.e. most healthful as if any alcoholic drink can be; he cannot explain why, so I think he is misguided as well. Still another is constantly searching for the 'best' vodka, defining 'best' as the crispest, smoothest, least aromatic. He finds one every two weeks or so and it becomes his house vodka until he finds another. The search continues and is part of the fun. In that way, at least, vodka drinkers are akin to wine drinkers.

Vodka is popular with tipplers around the world: More of it is drunk in Russia than in any other country, and, I guess, per capita consumption is far higher than in ours. I've heard from friends who have visited Russia that vodka is readily available and is inexpensive beyond our ken. Vodka accounts for 20% to 25% of all spirits sold in North America, and Vodka surpassed Bourbon as America's favorite spirit in the 1970s.

Perhaps its popularity is its potency: Its alcohol level ranges from 35% to 60%, perfect for a quick comedown after a stressful day at work or ball game. I think it's popular also for its lack of nose or aroma. Interesting that wine drinkers search for a pleasant nose and describe it with all sorts of adjectives such as woody, grassy, lemony, and fruity; true vodka drinkers eschew nose entirely.

28. Vodka, Shakespeare, and Job Security

Entire industries have been created around never-ending debates, aka differences of opinion. Some are useful and lead to constructive conclusions, others are downright useless and never lead to anything more than continuing debate and significant benefits for debaters.

Case in point: The debate over who wrote the plays and poems that are attributed to William Shakespeare has the life of Methuselah and seems so academic, aka futile. I have books in my library that 'prove' that those sublime works could not have been written by an uneducated clod such as the Bard from Avon. Ergo, goes the (fallacious) reasoning, the writer of such profundity had to be someone with more learning and intellectual stature such as the philosopher Francis Bacon or the noble Lord Essex. The results are huge advances and royalties for books that speculate but can't possibly arrive at the clear conclusion that would stop the unending flow of new books and new advances and royalties.

The martini falls in the same boat. Ever since Ian Fleming invented James Bond and Sean Connery made him the icon of cinematic cool, the debate over the martini has focused on "shaken, not stirred". Seems that shaking bruises the gin or vodka, which by implication is a bad thing. I have no clue as to why. Please help.

The Great Martini Debate boasts many other tentacles. Who invented the martini, a bartender in Maine or a bar owner in California? Should it be on the rocks in a squat glass or up in the classic fluted glass? Should it be garnished with an olive, lemon twist, or pearl onion (in which case it is called a Gibson). If an olive, should it be stuffed with pimento or garlic or blue cheese? Should it be dry, with only a drop or two of dry vermouth, or wet, with maybe as much as half vermouth?

And the big question: vodka or gin. The martini purist/traditionalist would react in horror at the very thought of abandoning gin and replacing it with vodka, as millions of tipplers have. Count me among them.

Countless books and articles have been written about the joys of the martini. The name itself has become synonymous with cocktail or drink and, of course, sophisticated cool. I've just added to the din, and expect many others to follow. Hey, it's job security.

VII. AVOID A VERBAL FOG AWARD

Introduction by Keri Cimarolli, Ecologist

Pete had one disconcerting habit when commenting on papers written by his students at Duquesne University's Grad School of Environmental Science and Management wrote for his classes. He would write "UGH' next to an error that he thought was so egregious, so disgraceful for grad students to commit, that we--his students --had to figure out what he meant and fix the offensive culprit. We could chart our progress toward becoming better writers by the number of UGHs on our papers.

He was a firm believer in Ernest Hemingway's rule for good writing: The first prerequisite is to develop an infallible, built in, poop detector. To that end, he started every class with 'blips of the week', errors that somehow were published in local newspapers, trade magazines, and, as we thickened our skins to better handle his critiques without crying, our own essays.

The UGHs evolved to become Verbal Fog Awards that Pete published on his various web sites, and nobody was exempt from receiving one. Pete especially liked to pick on journalists and politicians, probably because they were, and continue to be, an endless supply of raw material, as do attendees to his private writing classes that he calls 'writeshops.'

29. LOL on a Rampage

A friend and fellow wordsmith and teacher of wordsmithing who is as appalled at the current epidemic of bad writing as I am sent me the editor's column of a respected environmental magazine with this pithy comment: LOL!

I'm always up for a good laugh, so I read the column and discovered more than one LOL moment. The first was the subject itself: Carbon sequestration, which I think is much ado about nothing. The second was this sentence about a research project:

Initial funding for the project was a $600,000 grant from the Institute of the Environment's Initiative for Renewable Energy and the Environment. There was also a $1.5 million grant from the Department of Energy.

So I asked myself if the initial funding was $2.1 million or 0.6 million? Did the $1.5 million join the party after the party started? I asked my friend, and we're both scratching our heads while rolling on the floor.

I would have written: The project was funded initially by... (from here on I'm guessing, right?)

Then this editor compounded the felony when he wrote this LOL:

What else you got? *The above process is sure to capture a good volume of CO2, though it will not greatly reduce the volume of gas currently available in the atmosphere.*

Blast and egad, I thought. Why spend my money, and yours, to develop a process that won't lower the volume of gas (presumably CO2, but you tell me) in the atmosphere? Isn't that the goal? If he's referring to all gas in the atmosphere, woe is us! No atmosphere, no breathing, no life. And what does he mean with the boldface headline? It's gutter English, of course, that is out of place in a trade magazine; it also has no relationship to the following sentence, which is called a *non sequitur* in French, or 'it doesn't follow' in English, but how the devil would the editor know?

I can't help sharing this LOL from another magazine: *I grew up in Northern New Jersey, and I took a class in philosophy in my senior year in high school.* Drat those non sequiturs.

Darned if I can figure out the connection between where this writer, a professor who was explaining how he became a philosopher, grew up and a class he took in his late teens. Did he take the class in New Jersey or, say, California? The moon? (now I'm being facetious, and you'll forgive me, right?)

30. Laffable Lingo for Your Amusement ...

That's how a former student of mine and now a VP of a global consulting firm often starts his emails to me that he knows will tickle my fancy for blatant bullshit.

This time he may have outdone himself when he extracted this tarnished jumble-gem from a letter written by his boss:

A computer model allows us to chase full reality, but never quite catch it.

I immediately thought of my lovable and playful dog Korbin, who habitually chases her tail but never quite catches it. Doing so is her endless amusement and, at times, mine.

I suppose there's meaning in that sentence and, I'd guess, it's that none of us can depend on modeling to reflect truth, or predict the future with any precision. The writer agrees: *all models are wrong, but some are useful.*

If all models are wrong, how the hell can they be useful? Useful for what? Sending us to the wrong conclusion? I don't know about you, but I have enough of them in my life. (wrong conclusions, that is.) Next time my lady friend tells me I'm wrong, I'll tell her *but I'm useful.* Can you hear the stifled guffaws? The start of a marital spat?

Dick and Jane and Spot would turn green.

If you're as old as I am — and damned few of you are — you'll remember the tactful trio who taught us to read and write way back in the second grade or thereabouts. They would blanch and burp at any writer who matches a singular noun with a plural verb. *A computer model allow...* That's like saying *Dick and Jane allows Spot to chase his tail.* Or *Jane allow Dick to chase Spot.* Me Tarzan, you Jane.

And, speaking of chasing your tail...

When I ask my students why they want to be better writers, they usually tell me that they want to be better communicators. But, I explain, if you are a better writer, you are automatically a better communicator, so you are answering my question by rephrasing and repeating the same idea. It's called circuitous reasoning, and I wonder if Korbin understands it.

I think that she would. She was more in tune with my moods and feelings than any other living being in my purview. You can read about this marvelous creature in FINAL DRAFT: Just Add Tears.

31. Hype, O Hype, Thou Art Everywhere

We are constantly bombarded with hyperbole, aka hype — extravagantly intensive publicity or promotion, which is tantamount to cheating, lying, or tricking with words and pictures.

If you're like me, we expect it in advertisements. Nevertheless, I shudder when I hear that BMW is the ultimate driving machine. Whatever happened to Rolls, Lamborghini, and a bunch of others that I think of as more ultimate, if that is even possible. Does 'more ultimate' fall into the same basket of impossible conditions as 'more pregnant'?

And what about the Tesla 6, which Consumer Reports just named "The Best Overall Car"?

I expect hype in politics, a subject that deserves its very own blog.

But, dammit, I don't expect hype in academe...

...yet I get it too often, this recently from a professor of communications at the University of Michigan in an article titled DUMBING DOWN AMERICA, in which she proves that she is leading the way:

"Among the many visionary goals of the right wing--impoverish older people, starve the poor, deny climate change, outlaw abortion and contraception, eliminate healthcare for millions--few are more foundational than defunding education in general and higher education in particular."

I don't know anyone, right or left wing, who wants to impoverish older people, starve the poor, or defund education, meaning, according to my Oxford, to withdraw all funds, not merely to reduce funding. I do know people on both sides of the ideological fence who deny climate change, want to outlaw abortion but never contraception--we're too hedonistic for that--and wouldn't dream of denying health care for millions.

BTW, this professor wrote this to prove her point about defunding (obviously the wrong word): "... in Republican Gov. Rick Snyder's first budget, there was a 15 percent cut in state aid to universities and $1.8 billion tax cut for businesses."

Tell me, how many dollars were cut from state aid to universities? And is the comparison at all valid? What happened to parallelism?

32. Spinning as Lying? Does a bear...?

I admit it: I've been 'spinning' all my 40+ years as a writer of what I kindly call 'corporate gargle'.

By that I mean that I've interpreted, slanted, and bent information in ways that support my clients' purposes-- almost always a long way from truth. So perhaps spinning is a polite word for lying in a self-serving way.

Here's an example: The Duke University basketball team recently beat the University of Pittsburgh, 80--65. One headline:

DUKE'S VISIT A WIN DESPITE LOSS

Being the curious type--you know what that does to cats-- I wanted to find out how a 15-point loss can be a win, and read, mid-column: *Make no mistake, this was going to be a win for Pitt....a nationwide audience on ESPN saw the (arena) at its best and saw Pitt take the floor every bit Duke's equal.*

HUH?

Another headline:

DUKE TOPS PITT

Pretty tame, eh? A few games before, Pitt beat Clemson by a mere four points and the headline was:

PITT CRUSHES CLEMSON. So the Duke headline might have been: DUKE THUMPS PITT (Or CRUSHES or EMBARASSES?)

Both writers' agenda is to create interest in all Pittsburgh sports by painting them in the most favorable light; their careers are at stake. Can you forgive their spin?

Spin can be created out of straight-forward prose by judiciously inserting adjectives and adverbs. An engineer wrote this in his doctoral thesis: *The electrical power producing industry is the largest contributor of pollutant emissions to the air and water. Because of this, the industry is highly regulated at the state and federal levels.*

His agenda was to report as objectively as possible, so the words are tame. If, however, he wanted to bash the industry and emphasize the need for cleanup, for example if he were writing for an environmental magazine looking for ways to justify its existence, he could have hit a bit below the belt and said: *Power plants defile our air and water more than any other group of industrial facilities, a dire and despicable situation bordering on crisis. Therefore, and justifiably, such plants are regulated heavily and monitored zealously by State and Federal governments.*

Too aggressive?

A reporter wrote: Emissions of deadly carbon dioxide have more than doubled during the past ten years.

Now we know where that reporter stands on a controversial issue, and now you know where I stand. If he was reporting, he could have dropped the 'deadly'.

'Spinning' is a euphemism--perfumed, doctored language designed to make readers feel good when they shouldn't, and listeners feel good and buy the message and the product. Spinning is commonplace in the words of ads, press releases, editorials, and even reporting in prose. It is also common practice when reporting numbers.

It is verbal fog, and I want to eradicate it. Please help.

JACKPOT THREE: REMOVE YOUR TOXICS

Introduction by Stephen R. Covey, author of the best-selling book, The 7 Habits of Highly Effective People

You don't have to take insults personally. You can sidestep negative energy, you can look for the good in others and utilize that good, as different as it may be, to improve your point of view and enlarge your perspective.

*

... we are embedded in our networks of relationships ... perhaps the best definition of happiness ... and such a network cannot exist without effective articulation ... we listen to each other and care about each other's' feelings and concerns ...we label those who don't care enough to communicate well as 'toxic', and don't invite them into our inner circle.

From *The Power of Being Articulate.*

VIII. REJECT BULL*!@#. HERE'S HOW

Introduction by Gary Forcey, former Communications Manager, Westinghouse Electric Corporation

Pete Geissler has claimed often that he has written more than three million words for businesses that have been printed or spoken in formal settings. He goes on to say that 98 percent of those words have been lies, aka bullshit, but he has spun them so eloquently that only a few people recognize them as such. He is the pinnacle of bullshit artists.

Or is he? Many business executives, and certainly just about every politician, have shaped their careers around BS, just as Pete did. (Please recognize that I've just written an unsupportable generalization that could be BS in itself.)

Pete has often said that two of the several causes of happiness are, first, to recognize bull when it hits your nostrils, and second, to reject it for the noxious noise it is. Pete's book, Bigshots' Bull*!@#, addresses the first issue with a series of sniff tests, and the second with a series of examples. He also has written several essays on the topic, as follows.

33. Boisterous Bull*!@# : What's a Voter to Do?

Our so-called candidates for President are blustering boisterously as they shout, bellow, and gesticulate, hoping for your vote and ticket to the most powerful office on Earth. My ears and nose hurt, but nowhere near as much as my intellect.

I'm insulted that our candidates would think that I would swallow their BULL*!@#, and I hope that you are too. We can protect ourselves from the onslaught by recognizing a few nefarious tactics, led by that standby of fallacious thinking, *ad hominum*. The candidates are attacking each other rather than discussing the issues that need to be resolved, simply because the attacker doesn't know enough about the issue to address it with any substance or insight. Why be embarrassed by incompetence or ignorance when it's so much easier to accuse your opponent of the same incompetence or ignorance?

Then there's that other standby, the *red herring,* aka diverting a difficult or embarrassing issue to one that is simpler or, the attacker hopes, more accessible. One proposed solution to the seriously complex issue of immigration is to simply build a wall along the US/Mexico border and, in, in another example of fallacious thinking called *egocentrism*, aka self-centeredness, force the Mexican government to pay for it. That's still another type of fallacious thinking called *bullying*, which is too close in sound and spelling to BULL*!@# to be accidental.

And then there's outright lying as in the use of the word 'free'. For example, 'free' education for younger students is paid for by older generations that have finished their schooling, and soon will be paid for by today's students as they age and earn. A more honest word for this bit of bull would be 'deferred'. The same is true of any government program.

Sadly, our media choose to ignore BULL*!@# and print or mouth it as truth. As a result, politicians and others are allowed to get away with outrageous claims and statements ... and voters are in for a bumpy, contentious ride between now and election day that will be well greased by BULL*!@#. Careful readers will recognize immediately that the previous two sentences are in themselves BULL*!@#; they are another fallacy called *unsupported generalization.*

I delve into the fallacies of thinking in Chapter 38 and in my book BIGSHOTS' BULL*!@#. Both sources focus on the bull emitted by business, but the principles apply to any profession or person.

34. Boisterous Bull*! @#: What's A Voter to Do? #2

Our candidates for President, and, indeed, for any elected office, are still proving that they are shameless practitioners of *ad hominem,* that dastardly fallacy of thinking that attacks the person instead of the issue, thus evading serious and important debate.

Other fallacies of thinking also enable evasion and have surfaced recently. One that I addressed in Chapter 33 is *red herring,* aka diverting the difficult issue at hand to an irrelevant issue with more emotional appeal. Cruz and Trump played that game when they parried over the attractiveness and behaviors of their wives rather than their own qualifications to be President.

Another is *weasel wording,* aka being vague and general instead of clear and specific. Bernie Sanders fell, knowingly, I think, into that trap when he said, "The question is not what she (Hillary) says. The question is what her record has been and what she will do if she's elected President."

In essence, Sanders called Hillary's campaign promises blatant lies without using the L word. He also fell into the fallacy called *begging the question/assuming the answer* by predicting what Hillary will do if elected. Nobody is that prescient.

Both parties are guilty of embracing *observational selection,* aka enumeration of favorable circumstances or counting the hits and forgetting the misses. The Republicans are guilty of that when they boast that they are "the party of Lincoln", a big hit indeed. I've never heard them boast about being the party of George Bush. Democrats boast that they are the party of Roosevelt, another grand slam. I've never heard them boast about being the party of Jimmy Carter.

At the risk of fallaciously or facetiously a*ssuming the answer,* I predict that we will hear more of the same kind of BULL*!@# during any election campaign, and that you, the readers of my blogs and of my book, BIGSHOTS' BULL*!@#, will be able to separate truth from fiction, reality from fantasy.

35. Boisterous Bull*!@# And the Fallacies of Predictions

If humans can be certain of anything aside from death and taxes, we can be certain that we cannot predict the future with any accuracy or detail.

Our history is replete with examples; here are a few of hundreds: *Democracy will be dead by 1950*, wrote John Langden Davies in his 1936 book, "A Short History of the Future"; *Remote shopping, while entirely feasible, will flop*, pontificated Time Magazine in 1966. (Jeff Bezos at Amazon must have missed that issue.)

It will be years — not in my time — before a woman will become Prime Minister, said Margaret Thatcher in 1969; *Read my lips; no new taxes*, promised President Bush in 1988; and so on.

Despite the obvious failings and pitfalls, economists, stock analysts, businesspersons, and, especially, politicians, must predict, at times in the form of a promise. The results are often ludicrous, LOL experiences.

Here's one. In 1928, the president of a major company in Pittsburgh peered fifty years into the foggy future, to 1978. He boldly predicted that Pittsburgh and Allegheny County would unite under one government, planting his foot firmly in his mouth by adding: "which seems as certain as anything human can be." He went on fearlessly and foolishly to predict that a canal would connect the Ohio River at Pittsburgh to Lake Erie, all railroads will be electrified, and every able-bodied man would be licensed to fly a plane.

All wrong in1928, 1978, and now.

Politicians are addicted to rash promises/predictions. In 1970, Senator Gaylord Nelson warned that, by 1995, "somewhere between 75 and 85 percent of species of living animals would be extinct", without mentioning the consequences. I wonder what they might be. More recently, Donald Trump promises 'to make America great again' without revealing why it's not great now, how he will make it great or greater, or even what 'great' means. In addition, I wonder if actor Rosario Dawson was shooting from the hip when she predicted that Hillary Clinton could soon face an FBI interview over the email controversy while at the State Department.

Readers of my book, BIGSHOTS' BULL*!@#, can LOL while learning more about the fallacies and follies of predictions, and perhaps relate to Soren Kierkegaard's sage advice: "Life can only be understood backwards, but it must be lived forwards."

36. Numbers Don't Lie, Right?

Calvin Coolidge didn't say much — he was dubbed by the media as 'Silent Cal' for good reasons — but he is famous for saying that 'there are lies, damn lies, and statistics', establishing the hierarchy of egregiousness for what we now call, in our attempt at political correctness, 'misspeaks'.

Which brings me in one fell swoop to gun control without, I hope, starting a political brouhaha. I've read that some 33 thousand Americans are killed by guns each year, far more that the few hundred killed by similar means in other industrialized countries such as Great Britain and France. The reason supposedly is that guns are readily available here, and not there. Ergo, our government needs to control, aka limit, the availability of guns, presumably to those who will use them 'responsibly', e.g. to hunt deer and not murder people.

No sane person can argue against that, just as no sane person can dispute that our laws and commandments to prevent murder aren't up to the task.

But I wonder about the statistics and wonder if you do too. I wonder what the real national per capita rates are for us and other industrialized countries, which in my mind is far more valid than the gross numbers. And I wonder why the per capita rate in Chicago is highest among American cities when, I've read many times, the gun laws there are the strictest in the country.

You'll find a whole chapter in my book, *Bigshots' Bull*!@#,* about the misuse of statistics--the most egregious and powerful way to spew and spread bull. In it, I give this example: In the mid 1970s a client asked me to prove statistically that the world would run out of oil by 2000. It was easy: all I did was extend the contemporary rates of consumption and new discoveries and Viola! no more oil, or just a dribble or two available at sky-high prices. I totally neglected the law of supply and demand and its predictable way to raise the price of oil and, therefore, the rate of new discoveries. One result is the current glut of oil and its bargain basement price.

I wonder if similar forces are at work concerning guns. Several of my friends have told me recently that they are thinking of buying a gun for the first time, predicting that guns will not be available in the near future. I predict that guns will be available at higher prices, then the law of supply and demand will kick in again, just as it has with oil, and guns will be as endemic as ever and cheaper than bottled water.

Please tell me if I'm nuts, but not until you read my book *Bigshots' Bull*!@#.* I promise entertainment and enlightenment.

37. Apply the Three Sniff Tests

We're all faced with the very real problem of separating reality from bull: who can/do you believe, and what of what they say can/do you accept or reject? Here are three infallible ways to answer those tough questions:

1. Practice dialectic, the tried and true method that ferrets and tests reality via rational discussion by rational people who can shed their thinking biases and put their brains into neutral for however long they must in order to arrive at logical conclusions. Such discussions are so rare in these days of finger-pointing and self-aggrandizement that I fear that they may never revive. Perfect examples of anti-dialectic include the many talking heads on TV that masquerade as interviews but are really shouting matches with two or more people trying vainly to be heard when the din and acrimony guarantee that none can be. Sadly, the only practitioner of dialectic on TV that I know of was the McNeil-Lehrer Report, and it has gone the way of most sane and reasoned discussions. Many business meetings also tend to be

good examples of dialectic simply because one person is usually in charge and is able to direct the discussion, which may also be bias, egocentrism, or sociocentrism at their zenith. Be wary.
2. Understand the elements of critical thinking, a cognitive process that leads to rational decisions and judgments, and reject those persons who violate them, for they are bull shitters. There are at least twenty-five elements of critical thinking; I suggest that you read about them in pamphlets published by the Foundation of Critical Thinking, *www.criticalthinking.org*. Here are the three that I consider most important to your abilities to sniff out the bull:

— Be suspicious of purpose, since the stated purpose is rarely if ever the real purpose behind the message and is, therefore, bull. Good examples in business permeate the news, but they are especially evident in the pompous pronouncements that managing for stockholder value benefits all stakeholders and that downsizing is needed to save the firm, which of course contradicts every Bigshot's stance that employees are the firm's most important assets.

— Reject intellectual arrogance, because nobody has a monopoly on the one best solution to any issue and it pays to be wary of the person who says he/she has. Here's just one example in business that I have experienced: I was asked to write ads and brochures for a huge firm that wanted to enter a new market. When I asked what the firm brings to the party, I was told that 'we are ABC Corp and that's enough'. In essence, I was told to build a case out of egocentrism/egomania, which is always unsuccessful. Where's the substance?

— Detect media bias and propaganda, which covers virtually all of the media's pronouncements, aka. lies. Examples in business include the innocuous press release. It always presents one side of any story and it's always the one that paints the issuer in the most favorable light; is that egocentrism? Negatives are always ignored, which assures that balanced discussion is ignored. Good examples include the electric car and the compact fluorescent light bulb.

3. Learn Socratic questioning, which drills down into messages to find the real purposes, assumptions, points of view, inferences, and implications. I find Socratic questioning to be the close relative of the oriental maxim that you can't understand a subject until you ask 'why' or 'how' seven times. Terrific examples in business are strategic plans. They invariably focus on growth of revenue and profit, and Bigshots, when asked 'why? recite the mantra of most business schools that the sole or prime purpose of business is to make money, aka stockholder value. Of course, they cannot give the real reason: to grow their span

of control and, ergo, their egos and incomes — egocentrism at work.

38. Reverse These Fallacies of Logic To Rational Thinking

I know that I've touched on several fallacies of thinking — aka ideas that pretend to be logical but really aren't to anyone who can think analytically — in Chapters 33 through 36. Nevertheless, I want to dig a bit deeper so that you will question those who use them, for they are in the top tier of all bull shitters:

— Ad hominum is attacking the person instead of the issue simply because the attacker doesn't know enough about the issue to speak substantively about it. Sadly, our politicians and media at all levels accept this distasteful fallacy and call it negative advertising. The public follows, sheep-like, without recognizing that they are being duped, aka bullshitted. Ad hominum is often cleverly disguised in business. For example, when a Bigshot leaves the firm for 'personal reasons' or 'to pursue other interests', you can bet that the real reason, more often than not, is that somebody on top didn't like the person, not his or her performance, and engineered the exit. I saw it numerous times in my business career.

— Red herring is diverting a difficult issue to one that is irrelevant and simpler to argue, and which is the basis for many mystery novels. For example, a business Bigshot may state that the firm is environmentally responsible (an overblown or unwarranted generalization, aka a policy) and, when asked for support, state that the incandescent light bulbs in all offices have been changed to fluorescents (which doesn't explain the policy and is a minor and dubious benefit that anybody can understand).

— Circular logic — a.k.a. begging the question — supports an argument or position by repeating the claim in different words. In business: 'Of course our employees (or customers) are our most important assets because we wouldn't have a business without them.'

— Egocentrism is the natural tendency to view issues in relationship to oneself, to be self-centered. Managing for stockholder value is a good example.

— Sociocentrism is egocentrism taken to the group level. Labor negotiations are excellent examples since unions generally are focused on very real but narrow issues such as wage increases and job security, and companies on broader issues such as profits, stockholder value and, at times, saving the organization (another term for job security for all employees).

Egocentric and sociocentric thinkers strive to gain selfish interests (would Adam Smith be proud of them?) and reinforce their current beliefs; rational thinkers consider the rights, needs, and beliefs of others to arrive at decisions and actions that are beneficial (or at least acceptable) to most or all.

Other fallacies appear regularly. Be on the lookout for bandwagoning (arguing that a position is correct because so many people have adopted it); straw person (purposely misinterpreting an argument to make it easier to attack either the person or argument); tu quo que (justifying an action or position by accusing someone else of the same thing, as if that were relevant); and unwarranted assumptions (which cannot be supported by solid examples and which are typically based on preconceived notions ingrained by earlier experiences or egocentrism).

IX. HOME SWEET HOME IS MORE THAN A SLOGAN

Introduction by Bill O'Rourke, former President, Alcoa Russia

I was dazed by a series of family crises when my boss, Paul O'Neal, the CEO of Alcoa, asked me to be President of Alcoa Russia. He explained that the plant, Alcoa's largest, was unprofitable and awash in scandal, corruption, and extreme inefficiencies. When I accepted the job, he said, 'now I know that you've taken leave of your senses.'

Maybe, but I craved a challenge as a way to remove myself from my family's turmoil, and, in retrospect, I'm glad that I did. I quickly learned to appreciate the United States despite its many warts, and to pity those Americans who have never traveled to other countries but complain about the US anyway. I also learned very quickly that 'ethics' in Russia allows blackmail, bribery, coercion, and similar behaviors that we do not condone but are with us anyway but, I assure you, are far less prevalent.

I also honed my personal concepts of ethics and the need for and benefits of a principled life. As a result, I now lecture about ethics and leadership worldwide and have co-authored two books: T*he Power of Ethics* with Pete, and *The Business Ethics Toolbox,* with two professors at Brigham Young University.

39. To Russia, With Thanks

Some long-forgotten wag said that the worth of a nation can be measured by the number of people who want to live there. If that's the case, the good old USA must be a wonderful place; immigrants have been knocking on our borders for more than a century, among them, in the early 1900s, my grandparents and future parents.

If you need more evidence of how wonderful we are and can forgive us our problems, please read about Bill O'Rourke's experience as president of Alcoa Russia in the book that he and I wrote, *The Power of Ethics.* Here's a snapshot as told by Bill: "When I landed at the Sheremetyevo Airport in Moscow and after clearing customs, I was asked to put my one bag on a scale, told it was overweight when I knew it wasn't, and then told to hide fifty dollars in cash in my passport before being allowed to enter the country. I refused, which set off a loud shouting match. After a fifteen minute standoff, the extorter gave up and walked away in a huff.

"When being driven to a plant for the first time, the police stopped my car. My driver told me that it was common practice for the police to detain foreigners like me until I greased their palms. I refused again, so the police demanded to see my papers, hoping to find some discrepancy for which they could threaten to arrest me. I knew the papers were in order, so I willingly turned them over and, after a half hour of threats and grumbling, they allowed me to continue.

"When l arrived at a plant I found a mess that far exceeded my darkest fears: 40 thousand tons of scrap steel that had to be removed, accident rates that were ten times the average for all Alcoa plants, and fatalities that were common and accepted. Safety wasn't even an afterthought.

"Alcoa brought in substantial capital equipment via multiple trucks. One day the Mayor and his militia stopped a convoy and told me: 'I see considerable investment traveling through my city and I'm not getting any.' He asked for $25,000 before he'd allow the trucks to proceed. I refused, and, in another standoff, he freed the trucks 72 hours later.

"I could go on... the Human Resources Manager who extorted a part of the severance pay for employees we laid off ... the police who put a clear plastic bag of money on a sidewalk hoping that I would pick it up and they could threaten to arrest me when what they really wanted was to extort more money to not arrest me... and so on. You can read about them in our book."

"The culture in Russia is that if you have power of any kind you use it raise your income. I heard of emergency room doctors who extort their patients before treating them, and university officials who extort parents before matriculating their children.

"Thanks, Russia, for showing me why I'm happy in the USA and explaining why so many others in the world want to live here."

40. To Russia, With Thanks. Part II

In Chapter 39, I talked about the widespread corruption that Bill O'Rourke experienced during his three years as the first President of Alcoa Russia, and how he refused to take part. He explains:

"I wouldn't condone or participate in the corruption. I would periodically complain to the Federal Russian Government about the behavior we were seeing in the Regions. The government wanted foreign investors, especially Alcoa, to be successful. They saw our direct foreign investment in Russia as an opportunity to attract additional investment, and it did: Alcoa's can sheet manufacturing investment in Samara (where the 'best' can sheet coating line in the world is now located) attracted other can- making companies such as Rexam, CanPack, and Ball to consider Russia for their can-making plants. By sticking to our values, by resisting the illegal demands, we sent the message that we will not participate in unethical behavior. That message eventually was communicated and understood. Alcoa's investment was over $100 million in the second year and even higher in the third year." (Alcoa paid $257.5 million for the two plants and subsequently invested over $500 million for improvements.)"

Bill and Paul O'Neal, Alcoa's former CEO, infused safety as the primary goal of management throughout Alcoa, including its Russian operations:

"We decided to make safety a priority. Seven thousand employees were trained in safety in the first year. All employees were given safety equipment and expected to wear it. Compliance was close to 98% in the second month. We identified fatality risks – and found an astounding 4,000 in the first year. In the first full calendar year that Alcoa owned these facilities (2006) there were no fatalities. Now, these two facilities are approaching six years without a fatality. The incident rates (both Lost Work Days and Total Recordables) are lower than the Alcoa global average (of about 0.10 and 1.00 respectively).

"I mention safety because I see safety as an ethical responsibility of leadership. Sending our employees home in the same condition that they arrived is an ethical responsibility. Identifying risks and eliminating them, providing safety equipment to the workers, training employees on safe work practices are all signs of dignity and respect."

Bill, in his own respectful way, is quick to credit the Russian government for trying to change the nation's culture:

"I understand that the Russian government has recently increased the compensation for the militia and has asked them to refrain from their petty extortion, which has been reduced somewhat. I would like to interject that we can't be too critical. In the US, it was common a century ago to extort. It is still a practice in certain sections of certain cities. The Russians have only been 'free' for a couple of decades. Let's give them a little more time to right their ship."

XI. EMBRACE HUMILITY, ESCHEW ARROGANCE

Introduction by Martin E. P. Seligman, Ph.D., excerpted from his best-selling book Authentic Happiness

Humility, aka modesty, is one of the Signature Strengths of happy, enriched people. Such people do not seek the spotlight, preferring to let their accomplishments speak for themselves. They do not regard themselves as special, and others recognize and value their modesty. They are unpretentious. Humble people see their aspirations, victories, and defeats as unimportant. In the larger scheme of things, they think that what they have accomplished does not amount to much. The modesty that follows from these beliefs is not just a display, but rather a window into their being.

41. Identifying the Culprit: Arrogance

One sure way to destroy lives, businesses, entire economies and nations, and, in the extreme, the entire world, is to be absolutely certain that you can't.

Arrogant people typically make unilateral decisions that they are certain are correct and beneficial largely for themselves and, at times, for others, yet those same decisions often create the opposite effects. But they don't care: They are so drunk with their egomania, power, and influence that negative consequences never enter their minds; either the consequences will never be discovered or the perpetrators delude themselves into thinking that they are above reproach or punishment of any kind.

Arrogant people and their destructions are endemic, and they share similar obnoxious traits. They're unaware of the limits of their knowledge; they are insensitive to surrounding circumstances and their own, and others', biases and points of view; are pretentious and boastful and show it by pretending to know more than they do; and lack the logic needed to support their beliefs or decisions.

In short, they are so egocentric, so wrapped up in themselves that they easily, willingly, and foolishly believe that they are omniscient and protected from errors in any part of their current and future lives. They do not consider the consequences of their decisions and actions simply because they are absolutely certain that they are 'right' for themselves and, therefore, for everyone (their intellectual inferiors) who may be affected. They know what is best for others and impose that biased 'knowledge' on anyone willing to accept it.

Egocentrism is the root. Those afflicted with it judge the world from a narrow, self-serving perspective and typically are masters at self-deception and rationalization, maintain beliefs that are contrary to solid evidence, and violate ethical and moral standards while being perfectly confident of their righteousness.

A prominent example in business is Jeffrey Skilling, the former VP of that icon of abject failure, ENRON. He was so certain that he was more intelligent than anyone else that he belittled suggestions from associates, including those who warned that the illegal Ponzi scheme in which the company was engaged would eventually collapse, along with the entire company, needlessly destroying or upsetting countless lives.

Self-appointed seers display amazing arrogance when they announce their predictions with certainty, but are silent when their predictions prove to be off the mark. One of many examples from business: "there is no reason anyone would want a computer in their home', said ken Olson, top exec at Digital Equipment Corp., an icon that soon disappeared.

I witnessed arrogance several times in my career as a writer for businesses, and each time I was struck speechless, a painful admission for a writer. I was working with a marketing manager at a huge steel company to publicize a new, totally unrelated business: lending money to others to lease equipment and buildings. When I asked why anybody would want to borrow from the company, thinking naively that the answer might be lower interest rates or a willingness to take greater risks, I was told: 'We're xxx Steel company, and that should be enough.' I wrote a few meaningless buzz words, and was told that I was brilliant. The business soon folded.

I was working with a product development manager at Westinghouse in a similar situation, trying to figure out how to market a system to automate hospitals, a business far from the company's core expertise and strengths: electricity. While digging into why this particular system was better than competitors' systems, or even trying to determine if the system had a market, I was told: 'It's from Westinghouse, and we can create and manage any business better than anyone.' The company folded a few years later.

Examples in the military are endemic: 'Four or five frigates will do the business without any military force', announced Prime Minister Lord North on dealing with the rebellious

American colonies. Napoleon, feeling invincible after a series of victories, could not resist invading Russia, igniting one of the biggest and bloodiest routs and retreats in history. Hitler made the same mistake and found his Waterloo at the siege of Stalingrad and the subsequent retreat; so much for ruling the world and ridding it — in perhaps the most blatant and destructive display of arrogance in history — of undesirable ethnic groups.

Tojo, Japan's Prime Minister in the 1930s and 40s, overruled the wise council of Admiral Yomomoto and knew for sure that he could destroy America with his surprise attack on Pearl Harbor, but instead unleashed the greatest economic and military force ever created and he and the citizens of Japan paid dearly. And G.W. Bush knew for sure that shock and awe would defeat the Iraqis and they would welcome democracy with open arms. His blatant display of arrogance while declaring that the worst of the fighting was over on the deck of a carrier will forever stand as an enduring icon of self-delusion.

Robert McNamara didn't play favorites; he applied the arrogance he cultivated at Harvard and Ford Motor to the Federal Government and the military. His elaborate plans, dubbed 'systems analysis', for waging the Vietnam war were spectacular failures with one exception: they convinced the military that being flexible, able to adjust with changing conditions, was more successful than staying the course at any cost.

Perhaps the best examples are in government at every level and persuasion, but particularly the socialists and fascists who are totally convinced that they know how to spend your money and live your life better than you do. Examples abound and their destruction runs the gamut from local and picky to global and monumental.

On the local and picky side is the council of a small town near Pittsburgh that wants to ban outdoor grilling within five feet of a home, citing the need to prevent fires while admitting that none from this obscure source has ever been reported. Mayor Bloomberg of New York City has decided that you cannot buy a soda that tips the scales at over 16 ounces, arguing that he is protecting your health. On a national scale, President Obama has decided that you will fill your gas tank with more and more ethanol and spend your money to subsidize electric cars, citing the impossible goal of energy independence despite the obvious truth that producing ethanol and running battery-powered cars use more oil than they save.

Bill Clinton is at the core of this rancid heap: I feel certain that he never once thought that his dalliances with Monica in the Oval Office would be revealed and cause his impeachment trial by his many vindictive enemies. Could that one arrogant error prevent him from being lauded by historians as one of our best presidents?

In sports, Tiger Woods surely did not expect to be caught cheating on his wife, and when he was he lost many millions of dollars and the respect of millions of fans. Ben Roethlisberger, the Steelers' quarterback, followed the same path but, he says, is now a reformed family man. Pete Rose was caught gambling on the team he was managing, apparently not realizing the conflict of interest or, if he did, being convinced that his all-star status would shield him from any consequences. He was wrong.

Arrogance is akin to pride — the seventh deadly sin and the root and composite of all sins — with at least one possible exception: Recent research suggests that our brains are programmed for pride, and there isn't anything we can do to prevent it. Perhaps we are more in control of our arrogance, perhaps not.

I prefer to think that we can control arrogance with just a touch of self-awareness.

The three related traits of arrogant people; look for them

1. Secrecy

2. Unwillingness or inability to listen to advice from others who often know more about the situation.

3. Unwillingness or inability to visualize or project the future consequences of current decisions. (See Chapter 43 for more)

42. Identifying and Living the Antidote: Humility

Humble persons demonstrate awareness of the need to face and fairly address ideas, beliefs, or viewpoints toward which they are strongly opposed and/or have not seriously considered. They also demonstrate empathy toward and understanding of others by putting aside their own egocentricity. They avoid selective memory by thoughtfully considering and accepting, when appropriate, evidence from others that does not support their beliefs and decisions. They avoid oversimplification of complex issues and instead drill down by asking the why and how questions that discover a greater understanding of truth and morality. In short, they live with open minds and communicate openly and honestly.

Ronald Reagan fits that mold as well as anyone. No doubt his ego was huge, having risen from a lower-echelon actor to President. Nevertheless, he was humble in that he knew the limits of his intelligence and energies, surrounded himself with competent advisers, and listened to them before making crucial decisions—teamwork at its zenith. He also never wavered from his social and economic principles, igniting the most affluent era in the history of the world, benefitting his successors and billions of others.

A prominent sign of humility is interpersonal skills, as Daniel Golman points out in his book, *Emotional Intelligence*. He defines interpersonal skills as the ability to understand what motivates others and how they think and behave ... the capacity to discern and respond appropriately to moods, temperaments, motivations, and desires.

Jim Browne, a founder of a large financial services company, ranks interpersonal skills " most important' for success. He develops powerful and sustainable empathy with his clients by co-operating with them to develop their emotional quotient, aka tolerance for risk, before he invests one dime of their money. He is far too humble to think that he knows the goals and aspirations of his clients better than they do.

People demonstrate humility by their willingness to change in constructive, sustainable ways. It has been defined in other ways by many of the world's great thinkers, always as a prime virtue:

" Humility is the solid foundation of all virtues."

Confucius

"The first test of a truly great man is humility."

John Ruskin

"Better is to be of a humble spirit with the lowly, than to divide the spoil with the proud."

Proverbs 16:10

"Meekness (humility) is nothing more than a true knowledge of oneself as one is. Anyone who truly knows himself will be meek (humble) indeed."

The Cloud of Unknowing

"A humble person lives on earth as if in the Kingdom of heaven - always happy, peaceful and satisfied with everything."

St. Anthony of Optina

"True humility is not thinking less of yourself; it is thinking of yourself less."

C.S. Lewis, Mere Christianity

"There is nothing noble in being superior to your fellow man; true nobility is being superior to your former self."

Ernest Hemingway

"It was pride that changed angels into devils; it is humility that makes men as angels."

Saint Augustine

"Humility is like underwear: essential, but indecent if it shows."

Helen Nielson

"Humility and knowledge in poor clothes excel pride and ignorance in costly attire."

William Penn

43. Project the Future as You Must, but Don't Trust the Outcome

I have been fascinated for decades by The Law of Unintended Consequences, perhaps because it validates my conviction that humans cannot predict the future with certainty or accuracy.

Sociologist Robert K. Merton popularized the law of unintended consequences in his 1936 paper, *The Unanticipated Consequences of Purposive Social Action*. In it, Merton attempted to systematically analyze the problem of unintended consequences of deliberate acts intended to cause social change.

More recently, The Law has come to be a warning that intervention in a complex situation tends to create unanticipated consequences that can be:

— Positive, an unexpected benefit usually attributed to good fortune or luck (which can be tricky since there is some truth in the aphorisms that luck favors the wise and the prepared);

— Negative, an unexpected detriment in addition to the positive benefit, usually attributed to bad luck or fortune; and/or

— Perverse, contrary to the original intent, caused when the intended consequence worsens the outcome, usually attributed to stupidity or ignorance.

Examples abound. The automobile increased mobility, but its negative consequences include killing some thirty thousand of us per year on the highways and causing immeasurable environmental damage.

Aspirin alleviates pain, and, as a positive consequence, it also helps prevent heart attacks and strokes.

Very few people (some might say 'nobody', but that would ignore the few exceptions) marry to get divorced, yet, in a perverse consequence, more than half of us have been divorced at least once, which brings me to a personal story. I know a woman from a country in the Mideast who married an American solely to move here to become a US citizen, and then to divorce him after seven years and marry another American with more money.

Very few suppliers deliberately insult and alienate clients, but I did for ethical reasons and figured I would lose considerable business. Instead, my actions spread around the company and I was inundated with contracts from others who appreciated my courage and integrity.

Violations of the law are perpetrated by arrogance, as is unethical behavior. In both cases, the perpetrators believe that they can accurately predict future consequences (nobody can), and/or they believe that any consequences will be ignored or even accepted.

TRUE STORIES TO SUPPORT THE JACKPOTS

MY MUSE, THE BOOZE

"It's been far more glad than sad during the past 60 or so years".

I was rationalizing my habit — I'm too much of an avoider to call it an addiction because it sounds so destructive and would force me to give up my fantasy of enjoying, without guilt or bodily harm, the distilled grape, grain, and potato to the point of shameless hedonism.

So, as writers do so well and often, I justified myself even further: "Norman Mailer needed a can of beer to prime his creative pump, Irwin Shaw admitted that he got ideas while tipsy that he couldn't get while sober, Tennessee Williams couldn't write without wine to both kill and encourage his brain cells, Hemingway mixed bulls and tequila and wrote memorable books about war and fishing, Fitzgerald wrote wonderfully sensitive books and screenplays before going crazy from the hooch, along with his wife Zelda,

Faulkner admitted that after two martinis there was no holding him back and bourbon was a nutritious breakfast, EB White extracted the considerable courage to attack the tyranny of the blank page from a dry martini, and so on. I've done the same. Maybe if I drank more ...?"

A small, brown spider, the kind that bites and raises welts, hung by a single strand of its silk from the small balcony jutting from my second floor, swaying slowly in the soft evening breeze directly over my precious martini. Not housebroken, it had probably already peed or pooped in my hedonism, and now wanted a cooling swim and a quick buzz. I moved my glass.

"Famous writers, famous drunks," said my friend David, connecting the dots with his unerring accuracy as he listened to me muse about my muse. "Did you know," I enlightened, "that not one of the muses is dedicated to either prose or booze. Let's change that. I'll call her EraSot, the erratic but perfectly logical combining of the muse of love poetry, Erato, with my favorite persona."

David and I were on my newly scrubbed and stained back patio, sitting at my glass-topped picnic table under a large beach umbrella to protect us from the setting sun. We were separated from the current drug bust on the streets of Pittsburgh's vilified North Shore by a high, ivy-covered brick wall and maybe ten feet. We were doing our best to stimulate Poland's sick economy and our sicker egos by slogging down two of that country's most admirable exports:

Belvedere vodka, the grain kind and my choice, and Chopin vodka, the potato kind and David's choice. David was also doing his part to lead Greece out of its inevitable, socialist-imposed bankruptcy — the same road we in America are hurtling down with our extreme and shameful ignorance of history and economics — by adding three olives stuffed with almonds, pimento, and blue cheese to his crystalline booze. What's the global economy good for if not that?

I, a purist who is always on a diet, disdained all fruit. "Why add a foreign taste and twenty oily calories to a drink with the tasteless charm of crispness that is already packed tightly with more than three hundred calories?" Yes, I am no different than the Mister or Missus Obesity who drags their cabbage-patch kids under the Golden Arches and orders triple Big Macs slathered with fat-full mayo and diet cokes all around. If you can't stand a few contradictions, get out of America.

"It was a running back and a left guard who drove me to drink, and I never had the courtesy to thank them", I said, contorting a famous line from that most famous of drunks, W.C. Fields, after David asked how I started to love the hooch so much. "We — the three of us, blindingly convinced that we were the very heart and muscle of a stellar football team that was dashing to anonymity — we were on the front lawn of our high school in Ossining, New York, a little bedroom town, a whistle stop on the defunct New York Central Railroad that carried weary commuters south some twenty-five miles to their dreary drudgeries in some anonymous high- rise in New York City.

"Ossining's only claim to infamy, such as it is, is Sing Sing prison, the one to which the cops in New York City sent the bad guys 'up the river'. And now me, of course; I'm a claim to infamy. Not because I'm a famous writer or drunk, although in one of history's least famous drives to futility I've been trying my damnest to be both for the past four decades. It's my wardrobe. My youngest son has shamelessly dubbed me the Hugh Hefner of Pittsburgh because of my considerable stash of colorful and baggy pajama pants that I don for all occasions save the more formal. Hef needn't worry: The label hasn't stuck even among my closest friends and neighbors. As one said, I can't be Hef until I'm surrounded by beautiful and half-clad playmates with whom I'm shagging. Won't happen."

"Anyway, we were pretty much hidden on the front lawn by dusk that was cascading between some tall elm trees that were beginning to lose their leaves and those pinwheel seeds that they shower on the landscape in the autumn cool. Celebrating a win over a hated rival, close-by towns North Tarrytown or Peekskill if what's left of my memory serves after a million of these," and I rolled my eyes heavenward as I held up my glass to admire its dewy sides and promise of woozy and unfettered delights. "Sixty years ago, nineteen forty-nine or fifty, Harry Truman, McCarthyism, Guys and Dolls, South Pacific, Packards and Kaisers-Frasers and

Studebakers, Kon Tiki. All poof", and I snapped my fingers in the air. *The spider bounced on its string.*

"There's gotta be a schtory here," David slurred. He was well into his third Chopin and had dug down and pushed aside the ice in his glass with chubby fingers to extract and eat his olives to make room for three more. Rumors are that the Greeks, the dumdums, are planning to name their stimulus package after him, David-im-u-lus.

"Their names were Emmett, his real name, and Rooster, whose real name was Reuben, like the sandwich. One of them — I have no idea who — said those words that are sure to go down in history along with 'Give me liberty ... 'let's get some beer.' Come to think of it, those two famous sayings repeat the same noble thought.

"Please remember; I was a mere lad of 16 or 17 and beer had often crossed my impressionable mind — I had even heard that Ben Franklin had somehow decided that God had invented it, so it must be good stuff — but it had never caressed my lips. Honest. Nevertheless, the only thing I knew about beer and other grogs was what I heard on the radio and saw on billboards and read in newspaper ads. The Schaefer beer ads urged us to drink their foamy brew if you're having more than one. Now I know that nobody ever stops at one. And the Rheingold guys tempted us to drink their brew by plastering the smiling gorgeous Rheingold Girls all over. Yessir, we'd attract the great lookers if only we drank the right beer. Nothing's changed in the ad world, right? Right car, right toothpaste, right beer, sexy girl.

"Emmett and Rooster and I were the same chronological age, but obviously they were much older and sager when it came to worldly pleasures. They not only had downed a bottle or ten, but they knew where to get the stuff. So off we went down the hill towards the river and the prison maybe a quarter mile, to Spring Street. A little deli there that was owned by this guy who winked at the law in the name of a few shekels and sold quart bottles out of one of those white coolers with sliding doors for something like thirty-five cents, big bucks in those days when I was knocking down a buck an hour pulling weeds at the local nursery or delivering milk to the tiny houses for returning servicemen that were thrown up after the war.

"We pooled our nickels and bought a quart of the cheapest we could find — Blatz, Pabst, Ballantines, who knows? — hid it in a brown paper bag, and strolled with the nonchalance of big shots with a secret back to our spot on the lawn where we passed the bottle around. I of course had to act as if I was a seasoned drinker — you don't ever want to admit being a virgin in a cat house — but it wasn't easy. I gagged on the strange and bubbly and powerful bitterness of that first swig; I can taste it now, wanna spit it out. But I kept drinking when it was my turn at the teat, and it got easier and easier and funner and funner as I got dizzier and dizzier. Nothing's changed."

"So I reeled the mile or two to home on the hills overlooking the town, loving the feeling, as the saying goes, of wild abandon. Or, to be more poetic, loving that overly sedated sense of power and fame and calm and peace that we know so well. I was hooked on firewater; I was starting my march to the drumbeat of drink. Forever, and all kinds. I am free of prejudices; I love all booze equally." I bastardized Fields once again.

"Later that Fall or Spring, I was playing my beloved trumpet, a.k.a. Selmer, in a parade somewhere and ran into a bar when the pace slowed and picked up a slow gin fizz and was really buzzed by the gin and hot sun by the end of the parade… I was sloshed when our little dance quintet, The MusiCats, played at a fire hall and the beer and seven-and-seven were free … and I became a pretty steady customer at a small bar with squishy carpet soaked in spilled beer that was at 105 Main Street called, what else? Club 105. I can still taste the yeasty beer they served for a nickel a glass.

"If I got my bachelor's degree in drinking in high school, I got my doctorate at Duke University. I was a regular at a downstairs dive in Durham with that ubiquitous name, The Blue Note, and another in Chapel Hill with an even more ubiquitous name, The Rathskeller. Even their ambiences were so ubiquitous as to be endemic. You'd recognize the narrow stairways and low ceilings of their entrances and their windowless tap rooms that always smelled like last night's musk … musty, yeasty, the smell of an old motel room that had been used by too many guests-by-the-hours.

And I was usually first to arrive at our many frat parties held either in the frat house — violating all the rules against drinking on campus that were set by a blue-nose university still unwilling to admit that boys will be boys, and girls too —or in a place called 'the gulch', just over the university's property line that straddled a small stream in which we fell, laughing uncontrollably and often wrestling in the friendly way of young camaraderie, after we became properly smashed.

"While at Duke I switched from glasses of beer to pitchers and from sloe gin to seven and seven whenever I could afford it …then to that cheap drink known as Purple Jesus, a sickening mixture of grape juice and medical alcohol that we connived from the med students we knew. We couldn't afford gin, even rotgut or bathtub. "

"Us Harvard guys did the same …" David said, admitting for the first time in our long friendship that Harvard men had warts.

"I'll never forget my bachelor's party, two days after I got my sheepskin and a day before my wedding. I got so plastered that one of the bridesmaids dragged me under the dining room table, started necking and petting, and told me what a mistake I was making by marrying a woman who was dubbed Miss Iceberg. How prophetic. I could barely move the next morning and would have missed my wedding — think of all the pain I would have missed if I had — if my Father had not given me some sort of potion, I think my first

Alka Seltzer. Thanks dad, I think. Then when my bride and I were living in Durham we had a purple Jesus party and she, a novice drunk soon to join the pro leagues, threw up in the bathtub. Quite a mess.

"Too many frat parties ... too many boozy lunches and dinners ... and so many attempts to loosen my creative juices that two restaurants in downtown Pittsburgh attached brass plates — *Pete's Place* — to 'my' tables, and trained their servers to feed me wine and tapas as I struggled to come up with the grand idea for an ad or a brochure or whatever corporate gargle I was working on at the time.

"I guess EraSot broke my creative logjam more often than she failed. But I'll never forget a notable failure. I struggled while sober to come up with the grand idea for a movie, couldn't, and went to my favorite watering hole—another underground bistro, The Olde Allegheny, that was reached by a cramped stairwell, proving that history repeats like a bad cucumber on a rampage. I had tucked a few blank pads of paper to scribble on into my leather attaché, a gift from my Mother-in-law that was embossed in gold with my initials to prove that I was part of the corporate scene. Four hours later, totally sozzled, blotto, way past mellow and naively convinced that I am the next Spielberg, I went to bed in my downtown office. The next morning, head pounding and tummy grumbling, I couldn't read a word I had written, forcing me to recreate my scribbles of the night before. Luckily, EraSot rescued me and I was able to.

"Jimmy Carter damn near ruined my whole gig when he decided to 'frown on the two-martini lunch'; I'm ashamed to say that I voted for that killjoy, not realizing that he planned to ruin my lifestyle to pocket and waste a few more tax dollars. I and all the other folks I know who worked for themselves got around the law by playing with receipts."

By now the spider had mesmerized me with his swinging and had become my closest drinking buddy. So naturally I invited him to share my drink, raised my glass so he was in the ice and vodka, watched as he swam and, finally, drowned.

"How cruel", eulogized David.

"No better way to go", I slurred. "As Fields said, 'Drown in a cold vat of whiskey? Death, where is thy sting?'"

RAYMOND, O RAYMOND, YOU'LL NEVER LEAVE ME

One teacher, one career, many indelible memories.

"I just heard that you're a writer," she slurred as she approached me with that cocked-head and x-ray eyes look of curiosity and envy that we writers recognize from years of stultifying, but ego-building, experience.

We were at a posh cocktail party for some artsy or medical charity, and I was wearing my only dark suit, my only Armani as well, that I reserve for impressing the upper-crusters who go to such events. On its lapel I had pinned my caustic comment on cocktail parties, *Meaningless Chatter for Booze.* She was a looker, with the flat tummy and firm butt of a fit fiftyish that was a tribute to her personal trainer, and was dressed Talbot-stylish. She surely was a member of good standing in the exclusive club of Pittsburgh elite who appear regularly in the *Scene* column of the local papers. She held with proper delicacy and respect a half-empty fluted martini glass with a stuffed olive on its bottom in one hand, a wisp of her ash blond hair in the other that she twisted nervously as if she were approaching the pope or president, neither of whom I will ever be or see, and neither will she.

"You caught me, guilty as charged," I replied, stifling a thought that I stole from Bobby Knight, the irritatingly brash basketball coach who, in perhaps his most lucid moment, said about journalists, not us 'serious' writers: "All of us learn to write in the second grade ... most of us go on to greater things". Instead of blurting that bit of insult to my beloved profession, I switched gears to wondering why men never approach me with the same ambitions. Don't men envy writers in the same unrealistic way? Don't men want to write a book as their last testament? Don't men, except me of course, think their lives are interesting, exciting, enticing, and scintillating enough for a book that would be read by anyone outside their own families, if that? Don't men ...? I stirred from my reverie:

"It's obvious that you are wildly perceptive." Oh my, I thought, she'll see right through my sarcasm and be pissed and this conversation is over, my reputation in tatters. No such luck.

"Oh, no. I was talking to our hosts," and she nodded and pointed her Grecian nose to the well-dressed couple on the other side of the room, both with the silver gray hair that is the reward for the wisdom of age.

"I asked them who you are."

Being a confirmed narcissist, I was properly flattered that anyone would pick me out of a crowd of several hundred and ask who I was. And, being a confirmed bloodhound of bullshit, I knew what was coming next. I wasn't disappointed.

"What do you write? Have I read anything you've written?"

Anybody who doesn't know that writers write words is too dumb to be on my side of the tracks, but of course that wasn't what she meant. And of course she had read many of my words. She just couldn't possibly know that I, a ghost writer for those who are challenged by language but have somehow amassed the funds needed to hire me, had written them sub rosa, undercover, covertly, sneakily. So I jumped to the next Predictable Point:

"You've had an interesting life and you're either writing or thinking about writing a book about it." It wasn't a question.

"Yes. How did you know?" So I jumped to the next Predictable Point:

"It was a high school English teacher, and I never thanked him. Let me explain."

Her face drooped like a Dali clock in the desert heat. She wanted to tell me all about her interesting and traumatic life and what a swell book and movie it would make with Julia Roberts and Tom Cruise as the leads. She wanted to write about her three divorces and what rats and cheats her exes were and still are, her four drunken kids, and how she shagged the co-pilot on the cockpit floor of a 747 while on her way to Bali. She wanted to tell me all about her affairs with three men in this room and how they all were still in love with her. She thought that all this was rare, even unique and compellingly interesting, but I knew better. I had lived much of it myself, had heard it all from others many times, didn't need or want to hear it again. So, devious scribe that I am, I trapped her into my story.

"His name was Raymond, Raymond Hughes. He was ordinary looking at maybe five feet, eight inches tall and 160-70 pounds, a bit paunchy and soft and stooped from years of hunching over papers to correct and books to read. He was always dressed crisply in a starched white shirt, rep tie, and wrinkle-free dark suit. Fastidious. Could have been at home in a boardroom. While he looked ordinary, his passion for the language was extraordinary and it showed in his teaching.

"When he read the poems of the great romantics who lived in the 1500s and 1600s I could see behind his rimless, professorial glasses—glasses that glinted from the light coming into his room from a bank of windows to his right-- that he was so moved by the rhythmic assonance and lofty ideals that he would come almost to tears. He would shake his graying head with the dynamics of the meter until his jowls and dewlaps quivered under his ruddy skin ever so slightly. He was prone to the thunderous bursts of eloquence that evolved quickly to the barely audible whispers that only the dedicated wordsmith could muster. Fortissimo, allegro, andante, legato—he applied all the histrionics of music to immortal words. It's no wonder that Raymond is immortal as well, that he has been with me all my life in so many ways.

"When I am with my significant other I often think of Christopher Marlowe's *Come live with me and be my love, And we will all the pleasures prove* ...I like the pleasures part best." She laughed.

"And when I think of a former lover I am compelled to think of William Congreve and a couplet that is often mistakenly attributed to Shakespeare: *Heaven has no rage like love to hatred turned, Nor hell a fury like a woman scorned."* My one-person audience nodded; she had heard those lines, probably had lived them.

"When I think of my former wife, who is very much alive, I recall John Dryden's words about his wife, who was very much dead when he wrote them: *Here lies my wife: here let her lie! Now she's at rest. And so am I."* My admirer giggled as she changed 'wife' to 'husband' in her mind.

"I can't hear or read about a speech by our presidents Bush and Obama, and especially Carter, all master pettifoggers, without thinking of Alexander Pope's *An Essay on Criticism,* one of my all-time favorites. *A little learning is a dangerous thing; Drink deep, or taste not the Pierian spring:*

There shallow draughts intoxicate the brain, And drinking largely sobers us again.

"Speaking of drinking" I rambled on as her eyes glazed with restless amazement, "Raymond quoted either Jonathan Swift or Francis Bacon, I can never remember which, along these lines: *Drink, O drink, how I love thee! I would do anything for you, except die.* I'd wager that the writer of those deathless words soon died of liver poisoning ". I grinned and raised my half-empty glass of neat scotch in grave salute to a fellow hedonist.

"And when I think about quitting this delightful drudgery of putting words on paper or screen I'm reminded of an obscure poet named Sir Philip Sidney. He wrote in one of his sonnets, *Fool! said my muse to me. Look in thy heart and write.* Good advice for you or any writer or wannabee."

The lady was antsy, her martini glass in need of a refill, her mind in need of purging information she didn't want and couldn't process. She was in information overload and couldn't find the escape key.

"All that is nice but it doesn't tell me how you became a writer."

"In probably the most important way it does. Raymond's readings and assignments to read the romantics, including a heavy dose of Shakespeare, imbued me with a deep appreciation of the language and how it affects our lives in many ways from our wealth to our happiness. I wrote a book about that. But ... if you are looking for a more direct route from Raymond to my writing, here it is.

"I wrote a short story for his class—one of many but this one stands out-- that went like this. A mouse was gazing lustfully at a piece of cheese in a trap, longing to fill his empty belly with its fatty goodness. He knew all about traps, having seen his mother's neck squashed in one. So, in the true ways of mouse-think, he debated the pros and cons, the risks and rewards. 'I'd love that cheese' he said to himself, and 'I'm quicker than Mom and can outwit the trap.' It was the perfect agonizing of the antagonist and protagonist wrapped in one mind, just like Hamlet's *To be or not* ...

"My mouse went for the cheese and *snap*, he was a goner, again just like Hamlet and Ophelia. A fine story except I added a line about the mouse being dead when the *snap* said it all. Raymond caught me committing the venal sin of verbosity and wrote in red, 'What you don't say is often most eloquent.' I've never forgotten that—I can see the paper as I speak-- and I now enjoy a reputation as a concise, on-point writer, just what my clients and publishers send me fat checks to be."

"Whew", my newfound lady friend said under her breath with considerable wonderment, "You were very fortunate to have found and studied with Raymond." We parted, probably forever.

As she walked to the bar and a refill of her drug of choice, I knew that, barring a major miracle, she would never write her book. Only one of the several people with whom I've had this conversation came back to me with a manuscript, and she can't find a publisher.

I heard that Raymond had died recently, almost sixty years after he had changed my life and I'm certain the lives of others of my generation. He is plying his magic from his grave as I relive my short time with him by writing this feeble tribute. I wonder if he would approve of my choice of words and syntax. I wonder if he would enjoy what I've written here, if my words would in some small way add to the considerable validation of his life. I wonder if he would award me, a former professor of writing at two prestigious universities, an A and mark it with his red pen to improve it to an A plus. I wonder if I will always be his student, knowing that, yes, I would. Thanks Raymond, wherever you are.

BULL*!@# ETHICS RUN AMOK

Liz, a friend, burst into my home at 7AM, carrying her coffee pot, and, before even saying "good morning", said: "We won't pay your $1500 invoice for writing our website. Sam, our President, asked me to tell you because you and I are such good friends."

"Why won't you pay me?" I asked. "The invoice is four, five months old and neither you nor Sam has told me that it is unfair."

"Because we can't use what you wrote."

"Why", I asked again. "Sam was totally satisfied with it when he reviewed it with me right here on my dining room table. He even said that it is exactly what he needed and wanted; very complimentary"

"The person who was to design the site for a small fee didn't know how, so we fired him, and we can't afford a professional designer. We're talking to a student who may do it for nothing. So we can't use what you wrote."

"Not my problem. Totally irrelevant to my work."

"We overpaid your son for the photos, and I gave him two hours of free therapy on the drive to and from the plant."

"Still not germane to my work. I suggest that you talk to my son about those issues. He's 43 and able to handle his own affairs. Or, if you want, deduct $500 from my invoice and pay me the balance. Besides, although it's irrelevant, I charged you one-third of my normal fee for this kind of work simply because you're a friend. And you volunteered to advise Jeff; he didn't ask for therapy; you could have talked about sex or the Steelers."

'We still can't pay you . . . we're in a cash bind and aren't paying our suppliers. You can sue us if you want, but you'll have to get in line."

"Still not my problem. If you couldn't pay, you should not have hired me."

"Besides, you don't need the money; you have plenty."

"Still not relevant. I don't work for nothing and neither do you. Let's apply your thinking to you: You claim to be worth nine million, which I assure you is far more than I'm worth, and you have a million in your pension plan, and I'm betting you still expect to be paid by your employer. Besides, you have no idea of my finances, so you're guessing."

Epilogue: During the months that have elapsed since the above scene played out, Liz purchased a new Lincoln —

$50K? — demonstrating that she thinks more highly of her car than she does of me.

Liz does not come to my home for her usual morning coffee and has not invited me to any of her frequent parties, for which I am grateful.

THE BOTTOM LINE: Liz and Sam have behaved illegally (breach of contract); unethically (not paying me for reasons that are irrelevant and self-serving); and disrespectfully (my talent is valueless for irrelevant reasons) ... three ethical strikes.

THE BIG QUESTIION: Did they think that there would be no consequences of their actions? Did they really think that I would accept their behavior unconditionally? Is that the epitome of arrogance? (Yes, in my view.)

* *

JOBS AND SOCRATES

'I would trade all my technology for an afternoon with Socrates', Steve Jobs said, in October 2001, as he envisioned the classroom of the future. What could Jobs—one of the first true technologists-- learn from Socrates—often called the first true philosopher--or Socrates learn from Jobs, separated as they were by more than 23 centuries and wildly divergent cultures?

To start, they'd learn that they were avid searchers of truth and knowledge, constantly on the lookout for new ideas and insights that would explain their disparate worlds. They were avid champions for the powers of the individual and distrusted groups. They thought alike in many ways, and they expressed their similar thoughts in their own articulate words and aphorisms. Consider that Socrates pontificated that 'Wisdom begins in wonder', and Jobs echoed with 'Stay hungry, stay foolish', his prescription for the wisdom of creativity. Socrates advised 'Be as you wish to seem', and Jobs countered with, 'The only way to do great work is to love what you do. If you haven't found it yet, keep looking. As with all matters of the heart, you'll know when you find it.'

The similarities continue: Socrates said, 'The greatest blessings granted to mankind come by way of madness, which is a divine gift. ' Jobs said: 'it's more fun to be a pirate than to join the navy.'

'Madness' and 'pirate' mean unconventional, out-of-the-box thinking, another way to express the route to creativity.

Both eschewed dogma. Jobs: "Don't be trapped by dogma, which is living with the results of other people's thinking' ... 'Your time is limited, so don't waste it by living someone else's life'. Socrates had no dogma and Plato never mentions it in his writings about Socrates.

Both were autocrats: Socrates' combative teaching methods forced his pupils to realize their full intellectual potential and to open their minds to new possibilities. And Steve Wozniak, Jobs' partner, said.' I never really get to see, except second hand, how abrupt he (Jobs) is with people ...but maybe that's what you need to run a business, to find things that are worthless and get rid of them'.

And both expressed similar thoughts on death. Jobs said: 'Death is the destination we all share; no one has ever escaped it. And that is as it should be because death is very likely the single best invention in life'. Socrates was far more terse when he said: 'Death may be the greatest of human blessings'.

To love wisdom is to love both Socrates and Jobs. Both fought against sophistry, and both changed, presumably for the better, the world in profound ways. Socrates changed the way we think with his dialectic (and was unjustly murdered because of it), and Jobs the way we communicate and work (and was deified because of it).

I point out in my book, *The Power of Being Articulate*, that words can be used for good (think Jesus) and/or evil (think Hitler). Socrates and Jobs used their powers of articulation for good, and I am grateful for that.

FINAL DRAFT: JUST ADD TEARS

Korbin, my beloved WonderWoofer, was put to her peaceful sleep on November tenth, 2003, at ten in the morning at age 13 years, 3 months. My sadness is ineffable, inestimable, and inconsolable. She was, for twelve and a half years, my companion, friend, deepest love, and, I was fond of saying in an ironic truth, the animal with whom I grew closest. Lest I insult any in my army of two-legged friends (a category in which I include my offspring), I always add that my closeness to Korbin displayed some sort of character defect. How can a dog wield such magic?

Easily.

Korbin gave freely of 'unconditional love', a tired cliché that falls far short of what she in fact gave to all of us. She gave limitless love without reservation, and surely without that peculiarly human fear of commitment. She epitomized the disciplined generosity given for the sake of another that we associate with true love. Her life was an emotional give and take, an emotional symbiosis most of us search for and virtually none of us ever finds; she is to me the wellspring of poetry.

Nobody who knew her would find it at all surprising that we became joined at our emotional centers, became an empathic oneness, a phenomenon that transcended me to the hundreds of people who unknowingly fell into the irresistible, magnetizing force of her charm and formed her informal 'fan club'. All the members—and you know who you are—will always be her friends, and all of you are eligible for the adjective 'best'.

I could not miss her more. Now, as I write this exactly one week after her death, I see her spirit in every corner of my house. I am torn between removing the remnants of her life—her dishes, bed, crate, bags of food, leashes, cookie jar full of treats, rawhides on the living room floor—and keeping them so I can remember her more tangibly. I see her asking for a walk, poking her head around a doorway to check on whatever it is I'm doing, following me up and down the stairs to be sure that she never misses whatever is going on. I check the clock to be sure that I walk her when she expects. I wait for her excited bark and frantic dash to the front door when the doorbell rings. All to no avail: Her ashes rest on my bookshelf in a red velvet bag soon to be replaced by an urn shaped in her image. They are the starkest of reminders that death is final, and that the wheels of history continue to turn despite our deepest wishes that they slam to a halt, if only briefly. Suddenly, I am confronted and concerned with my own mortality.

She is, without doubt, embedded into my heart, mind, and the very warp and weft of my life.

She suffered a rocky start. Jeff, my son, in September 1990 found her and a sibling abandoned in a corrugated box on a street corner in Morgantown, near the house he and several of his fraternity brothers were renting. She was about six weeks old, so, a year or so later I very logically gave her my birthday and month, but not year, August 9, 1990. Anyway, Jeff and one of his roommates drove the two pups to the local humane society, and then, on the return trip, decided that the pups were too cute to leave to an uncertain fate. So they turned around, picked Korbin for her extraordinary perky friendliness (the other they think was adopted by a pizza delivery person) and brought her to her 'home' for the next nine months. There she lived an undisciplined life, with a diet of, I have said often with tongue in cheek but I'm certain with some tint of truth, beer and corn chips. The poor dog was not housebroken; she pooped and peed on the rugs and furniture, and she raced frantically from sofa to chair. She had no idea why she was being scolded, so she was confused and frenetic. The landlord, not surprisingly, was unhappy.

Jeff had no time for a dog—and Jeff knew I would disapprove of his having one--so he kept Korbin a secret from me, but not from Linde, who named Korbin Korbin after some friend at Sewickley Academy. Mom was in on the ruse too, and arranged to have Korbin spayed.

Korbin and I had a rocky start, too. In June, 1991, Jeff went to Wildwood, NJ, to work with a photographer, and I decided to visit for a week. We had a beery time, trying all the hot spots in that tacky tourist trap of a town. As I was saying goodbye in front of his rented house, Jeff, with perfect timing, said: Can you take Korbin back to Pittsburgh, and Mark Miller, a roommate in Morgantown and co-owner of Korbin, would pick her up in the morning and take her off your hands. I didn't see any option—the landlord had again struck and decreed, quite reasonably, that Korbin, who had broken through several window and door screens and, in some sort of gymnastic feat, had pooped on the roof-- had to leave.

Korbin damn near drove me crazy on the 7-hour drive in my tiny Geo Metro; she paced back and forth like a caged lion on the back seat, and jumped from the back to front seats hundreds of times, each time slapping me in the face with her tail, a habit she never outgrew. Anyway, I arrived home around 5 in the evening, just in time to go to Linde's graduation from Sewickley Academy. I dog-proofed my third floor bedroom and locked her in, feeling that my possessions were safe from her destructive teeth and claws.

Not so. She sliced my waterbed down the middle, much like a surgeon opening the chest of a patient undergoing a heart bypass. Then, based on the claw marks that are still there, she evidently decided to use the headboard for a diving platform. When I arrived home around midnight, she and the rug around the bed were soaked, as was the ceiling of the room below. Furious, I forced her onto the bed and into the water. She never went on the bed again. The cost to repair the damage came to about $2000.

Many people to whom I told that story responded, I'd kill that dog! Wrong victim, I replied. Kill Jeff! Korbin's OK, just confused.

Mark backed out of the deal to take Korbin—his father wouldn't have anything to do with such a gadfly. So I tried for about six weeks to find another home for her—I was very busy at the time and didn't need another distraction-- but the waterbed story and her general wildness doomed that plan from the start. So I resigned myself to having a dog.

I 'trained' Korbin with TLC and lots of it, and never, ever hit her. She became civilized, if not obedient. Mark Miller's father congratulated me several times for 'what I did with that dog', which was basically satisfying her needs and letting her know by way of positive reinforcement what I expected of her, and she told me what she expected of me. We settled into our routine: out of bed at 530 for a walk in the park next to my house, followed by other walks at 1030, 430, and 830. An occasional ride in the car, and all sorts of time together on my patio and in the park next to the lake, often with a flask of martinis or a cooler of beer for me, a biscuit for her.

Jeff, in a way, saved Korbin's life by adopting her. I saved her life at least twice more, when she ate enough of my carpet to block her intestinal tract and require major operations; the foot-long zipper scars were on her belly when she died. She ate carpet on at least a half-dozen other times, but I was able to force-feed her salted hamburger to make her throw up masses as large as a softball. And once, when Karl and Tracy were dog-sitting in my house, she ate the fringes off a wall hanging. Karl made her throw up, thwarting still another operation. We often joked that Korbin needed more fiber in her diet.

She had her mischievous side, and we can laugh about it now. One warm summer evening I was grilling two very expensive filets on my patio. When I turned away from the grill for only a few minutes, Korbin snatched both steaks and gulped them down, somehow without burning herself. I suppose I should applaud her agility and ingenuity.

Another day I was lounging on the patio and she wanted so much to join me that she burst through the screen door, which is still in need of repair. And then one day my assistant Dee cooked her favorite cheesecake in my kitchen, placed it on the table to cool, and returned upstairs to work. Korbin ate the center out of the cake, and Dee melted to tears. She forgave Korbin eventually, but I'm sure it wasn't easy.

About two years ago, sometime in 2001 I'd guess, Korbin's right shoulder became arthritic, and it was the precursor of her decline. The arthritis spread, and medications that squelched the pain gave her the trots. Soon, she started showing signs of hip displasia, and, in the pain that came through in her eyes, she lost her enthusiasm for her beloved walks and rides. She started to sleep a great deal and very deeply, with her eyes rolled back ominously to the gray whites. Then she decided to not eat her regular food, and subsisted on a few biscuits a day, then a bit of hot dog roll. She was not even enticed by rice cooked in chicken broth. She wasted from 50 to 35 pounds, and looked, as the vet said, 'pretty gaunt'.

A week before she died I put her bed and crate on the first floor of my house so she wouldn't have to struggle up the stairs. In the middle of one night just before she died, she did anyway; I like to think that she knew the end was near, and wanted to be near me despite the pain.

If you come to my funeral,

Come dressed in red.

'Cause I got no business being dead.

—Langston Hughes

I have relived the days and hours before her death a thousand times, and I always dissolve to tears and a bit of self-pity, and ask, why her? why me? That Sunday night I put her to bed, with a pan of her special rice, in my living room next to the stairs leading up to my dining room. The next morning, the rice untouched, she refused to get out of bed despite my enticing her with her leash and her favorite word, walk. An hour or so later, figuring that her sphincters were squeezing to their limits, I lifted her gently out of bed and up the stairs. Her legs splayed out as soon as she tried to walk on the slippery wood floor. She fell to her belly, then looked at me as if to say, please do something; can't you see that I am in pain, can't you see that I am embarrassed by my frailty?

I could, and decided to heed the advice of a neighbor: One thing we can do for our animals, she said, is to not let them suffer. What a shame that we can't do the same for each other.

I coaxed Korbin through her morning walk, then called the vet. I asked that Ken Bollins put her to sleep, reasoning that the person who saved her life twice also end her life. I asked that it be done in the car.

At around 9 I enticed Korbin out of her bed with the promise of a ride. I had to lift her into the car, and, once there, she took up her familiar spot on the passenger seat. She was alert—ears up, eyes darting--and I wondered if I was ending her life too soon. At the vet's, I asked if Ken could look at Korbin; I was of course hoping against hope for a magical cure that would postpone the inevitable, or, if that wasn't in the cards, I was looking for confirmation that I was doing the right thing.. Ken took one look, pronounced Korbin gaunt, and said that he had no magic pill or other cure.

Korbin was given a shot to make her sleepy, and we said our good-byes for the 10 minutes before the fatal shot. Korbin laid down on the seat, and I rested my right hand on her ribs, now visible through her thin layer of skin. I could feel her breathe, and, as Ken administered the next shot, I felt her stop and her life come to an end. Her eyes closed, and, I swear, she smiled and looked at peace for the first time in months. I will never forget that image, and I wish I could say that I take some comfort in it. I can't, at least not yet. I am still reduced to bleary blubbering.

Life often has a way of making people feel small and unimportant. But if you find a way to express yourself through writing, to put your ideas on paper, you'll feel more consequential. No one should pass through time without writing their thoughts and experiences down for others to learn from. Even if only one person, a family member, reads something you wrote long after you're gone, you live on. So writing gives you power. Writing gives you immortality."

— *Antwone Fisher*

My fondest hope is that these words that I have written will, in some way, lend immortality to Korbin. She deserves it; she has proven to me that only in the mysterious equations of love is there any reason for life, an insight that helps to replace the sharp sting of pain that I feel now with the countless joys that we shared during our many years together.

FURTHER INSIGHTS

On happiness

Authentic Happiness: Using the New Positive Psychology to Realize Your Potential for Lasting Fulfillment.
Martin E. P. Seligman. Free Press, New York

Emotional Intelligence
Daniel Golman, Bantam Books, New York

On creativity

Thinker Toys
Michael Michalko, Ten Speed Press, Berkeley CA

Serious Creativity
Edward De Bono, Harper Business, New York

On communications

Writing to Learn
Willaim Zinsser, Harper & Row, New York

EPILOGUE: WHAT WOULD JACK SAY?

"Crazy", that's what Jack would say. "Why go to all the trouble and hard work to change behavior and thinking when it's so easy to throw a handful of magic beans on the ground and grow a beanstalk that gives, free, no strings attached, a lifetime of wealth, happiness, and competitive supremacy?"

If only he were right.

Today, in 2017, we label Jack's magic beans a 'silver bullet' a 'quick fix', "the one secret to success', and so on. Our world is full of them and full of books and their authors who become motivational speakers that promise a bag of magic beans for all who follow the guru.

It's a hollow promise.

This book is not a quick fix; it is a guide to a better beanstalk. It absolutely will not grow overnight, and it absolutely will not yield gold coins, a goose that lays gold eggs, or soothing music ...all provided unknowingly by a generous but vengeful giant.

Only you can sow, grow, climb, and reap. Enjoy.

www.ingramcontent.com/pod-product-compliance
Lightning Source LLC
Chambersburg PA
CBHW031051180526
45163CB00002BA/781